# SPEAKING WITH STYLE

# SPEAKING WITH STYLE

## The Complete Guide to Public Speaking

**ASHOK MAHINDRA**
Chartered Accountant

**PHI Learning Private Limited**
Delhi-10092
2022

₹ 595.00

**SPEAKING WITH STYLE—The Complete Guide to Public Speaking**
Ashok Mahindra

Editor: Malini Sood
Social media: Aradhana Anand



**ISBN-978-93-91818-22-7 (Print Book)**
**ISBN-978-93-91818-27-2 (e-Book)**



Published by Asoke K. Ghosh, PHI Learning Private Limited, Rimjhim House, 111, Patparganj Industrial Estate, Delhi-110092 and Printed by Rajkamal Electric Press, Plot No. 2, Phase IV, HSIDC, Kundli-131028, Sonepat, Haryana.

*Foreword by*

**AMARJIT CHOPRA**
Chartered Accountant

*Messages by*

**J.M. SETH**
Chartered Accountant

**SANJIV SACHAR**
Chartered Accountant

**KAUSHAL KISHORE**
Chartered Accountant

# DEDICATION

I dedicate this book to all accountants who wish to improve their speaking skills and strive to be better communicators, be it whether they address boards of directors, committees, conferences, seminars, business chambers, regulators, or indeed any audience.

I also dedicate this book to all my former students in A.F. Ferguson & Co. Although they called me boss, I was the one who was learning and perfecting the art of public speaking through the numerous lectures and training sessions that I delivered. Thank you!

I also dedicate this book to all students, far and wide, who seek to improve their speaking skills. As the demographics in India are in favour of the youth, we have a unique opportunity to harness the potential of this young population.

I hope that those who read this book will learn to speak with passion and from the heart.

# CONTENTS

# FOREWORD

Chartered accountants have always been considered to be experts in the field of accounting, auditing, taxation, and so on. Ever since 1949, they have been able to hold their ground. Till the last decade, it was easier for them to do so in view of their virtual monopoly in certain fields, but of late they have been facing tough competition from other professionals like MBAs, company secretaries, cost accountants, and CFAs.

To succeed in a competitive environment, besides providing quality in service, it is also important to be able to communicate as to why society needs us more than others. It is unfortunate that the CA curriculum does not focus on communication skills, whether written or spoken. Generally, we find chartered accountants lack communication skills and are not good at public speaking. They may be brilliant technically, but are unable to communicate effectively.

Facing audit committees, boards, assessing and appellate authorities, and other regulators, and making presentations at times becomes a challenge for chartered accountants in view of their being communication shy and not being confident of their language. At times, speakers lack in content and are unable to make effective opening and closing remarks. In public speaking, it is of the utmost importance to understand the audience and to hold their attention during the talk. It is most important to close one's speech before the audience has lost interest in listening.

Many members of our profession lack confidence and are hesitant to speak in public despite their vast experience and knowledge. This results in society being denied the benefit of gaining from the wisdom of such members. Our professional brethren need to overcome this public speaking shyness.

It is in this direction that *Speaking with Style* by Mr Ashok Mahindra, a wonderful communicator and an eloquent speaker himself, will be of immense benefit to budding chartered accountants. I feel that even senior chartered accountants will read it with great interest, to improve their public speaking skills by smoothing their rough edges, whether it be in the area of content, style, or mannerism.

I commend the author for covering all aspects of public speaking. I am sure that the book will serve the desired objective and that professionals will gain significantly from the vast experience of Mr Ashok Mahindra. I wish the book great success.

**AMARJIT CHOPRA**
Chartered Accountant

# PREFACE

## As You Sow, So Shall You Reap

A.F. Ferguson & Co., a partnership firm of chartered accountants, were the defendants in the Tri-Sure India Ltd fraud case in the Bombay High Court (1985). Atul Setalvad was the leading counsel who defended the audit work of the firm, ultimately leading to its acquittal. I was one of the key witnesses to be examined. One of the primary reasons for me to take up the serious study of public speaking was that I never again wanted to be daunted by my lack of speaking competence before regulatory bodies and courts of law. My experiences as a witness in the Tri-Sure India Ltd case was the trigger that set me on my journey into public speaking.

***Why this book on public speaking?***

During the Covid-19 lockdown in 2020, I began going through my old papers when I came across diaries containing notes which I had prepared on the speeches and presentations delivered by me over many decades. The notes were highly detailed and systematically organized, and seemed useful and relevant even after all these years. I decided to use them as a framework for a book on public speaking, something that I had been mulling for a while.

The book you hold in your hands is the result. I present here the distillation of my personal speaking experiences, the methods and strategies that worked for me, and the lessons I learned along the way. Most of the techniques described in this book are based on my speaking experiences as a chartered accountant and subsequently as a member of boards of directors and of audit committees of companies.

This book will be a useful guide to anyone interested in public speaking in general. My purpose is to help readers become effective, confident, enthusiastic, and persuasive speakers. However, as it is written by a chartered accountant, this book will particularly appeal to students of accountancy and accountants in the profession and industry.

### *My launching pad*

The more speeches you make, the more polished and confident your performance will become. Seize every opportunity to speak in public, whether it be at training programmes, local forums, clubs, universities, business chambers, tax authorities, or audit committee meetings. Once you decide to engage in public speaking, many opportunities will come your way. Take these small steps and, by virtue of repetition and practice, you will improve your competency in public speaking. As your name gets known in the lecture circuit, you will receive many invitations to speak at various platforms.

In the early years of my speaking career, I took these small steps. I participated regularly in conferences organized by a leading client, DCM Ltd, speaking on topics that I was familiar with. This was where I cut my teeth in the art of public speaking. It was a wonderful learning experience, addressing small groups of known accountants in a convivial atmosphere.

My public speaking career really took off when I gave speeches in six cities in the United States as part of the delegation from the Federation of Indian Chambers of Commerce and Industry (FICCI, United States, 1993) to promote US investment into India. Subsequently, FICCI invited me to make presentations to business delegations visiting India from the United States, Australia, Singapore, Japan, and other countries.

Another great platform where I honed my skills was the Top Finance Executives Symposiums, an initiative of A.F. Ferguson & Co., New Delhi, attended by the top finance executives of the leading client companies in Delhi. These were full-day symposiums where the hot topics of the day were presented, discussed, and debated. I became a regular speaker at these events.

Another wonderful opportunity to enhance my persuasive and speaking skills was my participation in the Central Council elections of the Institute of Chartered Accountants of India in 1988. As part of my election campaign, I made more than twenty-five presentations to small groups of accountants all over North India.

### *Benefits of public speaking*

In many situations, the person who speaks best has a considerable advantage over others, and usually ends up ahead in the race for promotions and success. Leadership positions come more easily to those who have the ability to make powerful presentations. If you want to get ahead and be noticed, public speaking will help you do just that. Failure to communicate effectively can hold you back professionally, and even personally. The ability to speak well and present your point of view clearly, persuasively, and memorably will benefit you throughout your life.

More importantly, effective communication is not about being a smooth or glib talker. It is not about mastering PowerPoint presentations. It is not about citing facts, figures, and statistics. Instead, it is about engagement and empathy. It is about reaching out with sincerity and authenticity to your audience, and conveying a message that touches both the hearts and minds of listeners. The French proverb sums it up well: 'Great thoughts always come from the heart.'

To the extent that the ideas presented here will help students, accountants, and others who read this book realize their leadership aspirations through speaking with style, the book will have served its purpose. As appetite grows with eating, so interest will increase with accomplishment.

### *Organization of chapters*

The book has six parts:

- Preparation
- Presentation
- Words and rhetorical devices
- Self-analysis
- Regulatory bodies and law courts
- Conclusion

There are sixty-five chapters. Each chapter is self-contained and complete in itself. Most of the chapters cover a technique that once mastered will enhance your power as a speaker.

Some readers may find that making eye contact or adopting a proper stance is more difficult than some other techniques. That is perfectly normal. Giving a memorable speech does not require you to be 100 per cent proficient in every one of the procedures described in this book. So long as you grasp the overall idea and adopt a mix of strategies, you will be able to improve your skills.

### *There are three ways of reading this book*

- Reading from the beginning to the end in sequential order
- Reading the chapters at random
- Skimming through and reading what interests you

For those just beginning their journey in public speaking, you could select some methods from certain chapters and spend time rehearsing them and incorporating them in your speaking style. For example, you could pick six chapters at random, say, those on stories, stance, eye contact, pause, smile, and alliteration. You could adopt the practices described in these chapters and successfully apply them in your next speech. For the speeches that follow, you could select another group of tactics from another set of chapters and incorporate them in your speaking style. In this manner, you will be able to cover all the methods described in this book. This step-by-step learning process is easy because it breaks up the task into manageable chunks.

For more experienced public speakers, some of you may choose to move through the book more rapidly, skimming over what you already know and only paying attention to what interests you the most. This is a quick and easy way for more seasoned speakers to identify and fix certain problems or weaknesses in their speaking style.

### *These techniques have worked for me*

These are practically applied methods and have worked for me, and they will certainly work for you as well. Adopting them requires dedication and hard work, but the investment in time and effort is worth it, because you will reap a double benefit. These methods will boost your confidence, improve your personality, and create leadership positions for you. As your self-assurance and poise increase with each speech, your entire personality will come into its own. You will feel better both emotionally and physically. You will experience a lifting of the spirits, a sense of well-being, and pride in your accomplishments like never before.

Speaking with style is not a matter of chance, or luck, or just winging it; it is a matter of choice and deliberation, of preparation and study, of practice and rehearsal. As you sow, so shall you reap.

### *Deeply honoured*

To those who have purchased this book, I am deeply honoured by your decision to invest your time in reading my book. I want you to know how personal this is for me. I give you here the best of my personal speaking experiences extending over forty years. Thank you for allowing me the privilege of sharing my adventures in public speaking with you and a chance to make a difference in your life.

**Ashok Mahindra**

# MESSAGE

**J.M. SETH**
Chartered Accountant

It is my pleasure to write this message on Speaking with Style by Ashok Mahindra, a highly skilled speaker.

Apart from my long association with Ashok Mahindra in A.F. Ferguson/Deloitte, he has been my mentor, guide, and friend.

It is generally believed that accountants, in spite of having superior technical knowledge, do not do well in communication and presentations as compared to MBAs, particularly in today's business and professional world where there is a lot of thrust on how to communicate well and use positive body language.

I know that it has always been Ashok Mahindra's passion to impart knowledge and training to accountants in this area in order to improve their communication skills. I recollect that immediately on our retirement in 2008 (both of us retired on the same date), he mooted the idea to me and the late Mr Amal Ganguli, former managing partner of PricewaterhouseCoopers, at a luncheon meeting at his Delhi residence, of forming a special forum to impart speaking skills to accountants, but somehow that idea could not be taken forward.

His authoring of this eloquent book on speaking skills for accountants now is certainly not a surprise to me. It has always been his long-cherished desire which he has now accomplished in the form of this book, *Speaking with Style.*

This comprehensive book provides an extremely effective approach to public speaking. All the pages are imbued with wisdom and are born out of many years of personal experience in tackling public speaking techniques in a practical manner. It is very well structured, so that the entire speaking strategy is built one step upon another in a very helpful way. The language is plain and the ideas are expressed with clarity and precision and with ample examples and illustrations. The structure of the chapters is rationally planned.

It starts with the most important item—the audience—and the need for conducting an audience analysis beforehand, that is, understanding to whom one will be communicating the message. This is essential not only from the point of view of delivering a speech but also from the point of view of effectively conducing all other kinds of communications in important meetings.

The next item is the structure of the message that is planned to be communicated. Ashok Mahindra explains this nicely through the analogy of 'railway wagons held together by couplings', with the couplings representing transitions from one point to the next. Simultaneously, he cautions us not to 'emulate the mountain goat by meandering all over'. He advocates that we follow a definite structure, with breaks and recaps, make a few points only, and support each idea with examples, illustrations, and specifics.

Ashok Mahindra emphasizes the use of appropriate words in a speech to make a memorable impact on the audience. He has especially crafted eleven chapters in Part III: 'Words and rhetorical devices' that are very interesting. Many speakers will appreciate these rhetorical devices and may be tempted to use them in their next speech. Mainly, they are: antithesis, anaphora, hypophora, asyndeton, hyperbole, litotes, simile, and metaphor.

Structure, breaks, recaps, pauses, phrases, specifics, stories, gestures, smile, eye contact, stance, body language, humour, wit, voice, and tone are all part of the overall presentation, which makes the listening experience a pleasure. It is to be noted, as Ashok Mahindra points out, that personal and inspirational stories hold the audience's attention.

In the context of the importance of recaps, he cites a most helpful instruction: 'Tell them what you're going to tell them; next, tell them; next, tell them what you told them.' In this manner, one leaves a lasting impact on the audience.

Delivery is the final item of eloquence. It requires practice, discipline, and drill, and becoming your own trainer. While emphasizing the importance of delivery, Ashok Mahindra draws our attention to the 80/20 principle. As you are communicating to the audience, you have to make sure that you reach them definitely. Therefore, your efforts only to the extent of 20 per cent should be on 'gathering the material' and 80 per cent should be on 'delivery'.

For delivery, Ashok Mahindra emphasizes that one has to practise, practise, practise—rehearsing by day and letting ideas brew by night. There is no escape from practice. It will assist one in extempore speeches, a preferred form for highly effective communication. In spite of being a skilled and highly effective speaker himself, the author used to rehearse at least twelve times for each speech. He recommends against memorizing a speech, because, as he points out, there is a danger of forgetting. He gives the example of what happened to Winston Churchill when he decided to go in for a memorized speech before the British Parliament, but forgot his lines in between and had to sit down in embarrassment.

Further, for extempore speeches, Ashok Mahindra recommends the use of prompt cards, where minimum information is noted down on cards to assist the speaker.

He suggests that speakers should think of incorporating the elements of ethos, logos, and pathos in the contents of their speeches to make them memorable.

Having regard to his experience of handling regulators during his long career, he has included Part V: 'Regulatory bodies and law courts', which will be very helpful to readers, particularly to accountants.

For the guidance of readers, Ashok Mahindra has shared some important extracts from the speeches of great speakers like Lincoln, Churchill, Kennedy, and Nehru.

My recommendation to readers is to definitely read the chapters on the eight techniques that play a key role in public speaking and the three pillars for laying a solid foundation for successful speaking, as discussed in detail in Chapter 65, 'Magic list for excellence in public speaking'.

I am of the firm view that *Speaking with Style* is a true gift to accountants who want to become highly effective and powerful speakers.

# MESSAGE

**SANJIV SACHAR**
*Chartered Accountant*

The most valuable asset for professionals is their reputation. It takes decades to build one, and even a minor lapse can erode it in a few minutes. This was the key learning for me during my articleship training at A.F. Ferguson, Chartered Accountants, where I was guided and mentored by AKM, as Mr Ashok K. Mahindra is addressed by his mentees and friends.

AKM has very rightly chosen the important subject of public speaking for his book, since it is critical that we professionals give equal importance to improving our communication skills as much as we do to enhancing our technical knowledge if we want to be at the forefront in leading organizations and be seen as inspirational leaders.

AKM's unique style of narrating his real-life experiences, and making them reference points for sharing his knowledge and best practices, makes reading the book highly engaging. Another unique aspect of this book is the simplicity and detailed orientation with which AKM guides us on how to prepare for diverse public speaking opportunities like presentations to boards, workshops, conferences, interactions with regulators, etc. It will become your constant companion for your various speaking engagements.

When we think of professionals who inspire us very day to deliver our best, we observe that not only do they put in long hours of hard work and have a strong value system, but they are also highly articulate and confident in expressing their views and thoughts, which are backed by in-depth knowledge and experience, to a diverse set of stakeholders.

AKM's book is a must-read and knowledge repository for all professionals, whether you are just starting your career or managing a leadership role or even leading a quiet life post retirement. Wishing AKM the very best in his new avatar as an author.

# MESSAGE

**KAUSHAL KISHORE**
*Chartered Accountant*

I distinctly remember Ashok Mahindra's usage of fundamentals in one of his speeches that I attended in the initial days of my career. I learnt the three essentials of any speech: 'Tell them what you're going to tell them; next, tell them; next, tell them what you told them.' The concept has never faded from my mind. The author is a master of such fundamentals.

I have known Ashok Mahindra for more than twenty-five years, and this book epitomizes his pursuit of quality, clarity, and simplicity in articulation and communication. 'Learn to speak with passion and from your heart' is an overarching message for a good public speaker.

A genuine reflection of walking the talk, the author has shared invaluable practical experiences, truly lived over decades. There can't be a better foundation for a book than his notes preserved in diaries and systematically maintained, based on the practical experiences of speeches given over many decades and now converted into a book. Clearly, this is an excellent framework based on time-tested recipes on public speaking.

The book teaches how to challenge oneself by venturing into the uncomfortable and the unknown. The 'do not quit' attitude has been demonstrated convincingly.

I note a few prominent messages from the book, for example, 'Through small steps in speaking and by virtue of repetition, one will improve competency in public speaking.' Also, 'It is not about citing facts, figures, and statistics. Instead, it is about engagement and empathy. It is about reaching out with sincerity and authenticity to your audience, and conveying a message that touches both the hearts and minds of listeners.'

Fundamentals don't change. There are no alternatives to the basic principles of knowing your audience and ensuring an adequate level of preparation. Also, continuing self-assessment and the habit of self-correction are essential.

This book is not just for accountants. There is something useful that every professional may extract from this book.

It covers a wide spectrum of experiences, ranging from providing technical training to accountancy students, participating in high-class forums of elite professionals, convincing business delegations and the investor community, deliberating on taxation and other policy matters, defending professional positions in a court of law, and addressing forums on the conservation of wildlife.

*Speaking with Style* has such an amazing, lucid flow that even if one reads the chapters at random, it is equally advantageous.

# ACKNOWLEDGEMENTS

The public speaker seeks to reach out to the audience with sincerity and humility, striving to establish a rapport and hoping that the message will resonate with listeners. The audience returns the speaker's diligence and dedication with their attention and pin drop silence. When both speaker and listeners connect and are simpatico, the result is an intimate feeling of warmth, sharing, and understanding. This generates a certain something—an appealing quality, a wonderful feeling—that cannot be adequately described or expressed—what the French call *je ne sais quoi.*

I acknowledge all my audiences, from the smallest to the largest, who have heard me out over four decades with patience, appreciation, and often generous applause. Thank you very much.

**Ashok Mahindra**

# ABOUT THE AUTHOR

Ashok Mahindra has delivered many speeches to different audiences and on diverse topics over the last forty years, from 1980 to 2020. He defines speechmaking as the ability to reach out to and connect with audiences through a variety of multisensory experiences.

In this book, he shares his personal experiences of making speeches; discusses appearing as a key witness for the defendants in the Tri-Sure India Ltd fraud case which led him to seriously pursue the art of public speaking; his most difficult audience analysis; and his most challenging speaking assignment. Based on his speaking experiences, he provides a magic list of techniques for excellence in public speaking.

This book will be of interest to all those who want to excel in the art of making speeches, and will be particularly useful for students of accountancy, accountants in practice and industry, and other professionals.

Ashok Mahindra was educated at Doon School, Dehradun, India; St. Stephen's College, Delhi University, India; and St. John's College, Oxford University, UK. He attended Oxford University on a Burmah-Shell Scholarship.

After his MA in Philosophy, Politics, and Economics (PPE), he joined Chalmers, Impey & Co., London, UK to serve his articles to become a chartered accountant. He returned to India in 1969 and joined A.F. Ferguson & Co. as a principal in their Mumbai office and worked under senior partner K.R. Alpaiwalla. Several years later, he was posted to the Delhi office where he worked under senior partner R.S. Subramaniam.

Ashok Mahindra's career as a chartered accountant spanned thirty-nine years, from 1969 to 2008. He retired as Co-Chairman, Deloitte, Haskins & Sells, India and Senior Partner, A.F. Ferguson & Co., India.

He also held positions as Independent Director & Chairman of the Audit Committee of Nestlé India Ltd and as Treasurer Trustee and Vice-President of WWF-India.

He is a Fellow member of the Institute of Chartered Accountants of India, the Institute of Chartered Accountants in England and Wales, and the Chartered Institute of Taxation, UK.

Ashok Mahindra is currently engaged in wildlife conservation and philanthropy. He is an avid photographer and keen traveller. He advocates and supports the protection of wildlife and wildlife habitat through the Hem Chand Mahindra Foundation.

To know more about Ashok Mahindra, visit www.wildlifephotographybyakm.com

# SPEAKING STRATEGY

## *Move from Familiar to Unfamiliar Topics and from Known to Unknown Audiences*

***Develop a speaking strategy***

Once I had decided to enhance my speaking skills, I developed a speaking strategy and went about the task in a well-thought-out and structured manner along the following lines:

- In-house training workshops at the firm where I was a partner, A.F. Ferguson & Co. (AFF)
- Study groups of the Institute of Chartered Accountants of India (ICAI)
- Conferences organized by the Northern India Regional Council (NIRC) of ICAI
- All-India seminars on tax and company law organized by ICAI
- All-India conferences of chartered accountants organized by ICAI
- Conferences organized by the South Asian Federation of Accountants (SAFA)
- Other diverse forums like the Top Delhi Finance Executives Symposium; Shri Ram College of Commerce, University of Delhi; Delhi Management Association; Management Development Institute; Central Board of Direct Taxes; Ghaziabad Tax Bar Association; Institute of Internal

Auditors; Institute of Company Secretaries of India; National Conservation Congress; World Wide Fund for Nature; French Embassy in India; and more.

- Business chambers like the Federation of Indian Chambers of Commerce and Industry (FICCI), the Associated Chambers of Commerce and Industry of India (ASSOCHAM), and the Indo-American Chamber of Commerce (IACC). I made presentations to business delegations from the United States, Japan, Singapore, Australia, and other countries.
- Talks on tax and other related topics for accounting and consulting firms
- Television appearances on tax-related matters
- Business presentations
- Board of directors and audit and other committee meetings
- Partners' conferences of AFF and Deloitte, India
- Speaking events in foreign locations like the United States, the United Kingdom, Israel, Dubai, Nepal, and Pakistan

I started out with forums of the ICAI: study groups, NIRC, all-India seminars, and finally all-India conferences. Every city has various forums, clubs, associations, and institutes that provide an opportunity for delivering speeches. I used the Delhi Management Association, the Ghaziabad Tax Bar Association, the Management Development Institute, and others for this purpose. Chambers of business provide another fertile ground for honing one's skills in the art of public speaking. I made myself available to FICCI for business presentations to visiting foreign delegations. Audit committee meetings of companies are another forum where you can improve your oratorical skills.

### *Move from the familiar to the unfamiliar*

You will notice that as part of my strategy, I started out by speaking on familiar topics, matters relating to my field of accountancy, and by addressing familiar audiences like my staff and clients. I then moved on to unfamiliar topics like promoting investments into India, and unfamiliar audiences in foreign countries. As you gain experience in public speaking, you scale up from familiar topics to unfamiliar topics, and from known audiences to unknown audiences.

Begin in a small manner with the familiar—familiar topics, familiar audiences, familiar organizers, and familiar locations. Then, after you have accumulated sufficient experience by undertaking several successful speaking engagements, move to the unknown. Move to more challenging speaking engagements, to unfamiliar topics, unfamiliar audiences, unfamiliar organizers, and unfamiliar locations.

### *Pre- and post-2008*

Until I retired in 2008, my speeches were almost exclusively on audit, tax, consultancy, internal controls, frauds, regulators, governance, business and investment opportunities in India, and so on. I hope that I was accepted by my audiences as knowledgeable on these topics. After my retirement, my speeches have focused more on conservation, the environment, and wildlife. In both cases, the techniques for good speaking remain the same.

### *Break your big goals into smaller goals*

Remember mastering the art of public speaking is not so easy. It is learned with constant practice. It comes from searching for and accepting speaking engagements. It comes from having a speaking strategy—a speaking goal. It comes from stretching your communication style from easy to more challenging. To increase your abilities, you will have to challenge yourself by venturing into the uncomfortable, the unknown, and the unfamiliar.

Break your big goals into smaller goals. Smaller goals are less daunting and easier to achieve than a large, overly ambitious goal.

Persist and do not quit. If you face some initial obstacles, learn to overcome them. Adapt, experiment, and push on. The more speeches you make, the more solid your foundation and the more polished your performance are likely to become. You do not need to attend a lot of expensive seminars on public speaking. If you want to get better, just accept more speaking engagements.

### *Finally*

As you make speeches more often, you get over your fear of public speaking; you gain confidence; and with confidence comes eventually mastery. It is a matter of habit, repetition, and constant practice. Soon you will discover, as countless other speakers have done, that by building a record of successful speaking engagements and by gaining a reputation as an interesting and compelling speaker, public speaking becomes a pleasure and a joy. Follow where the path may lead and where there is no path, carve out your own trail.

# Part One

# PREPARATION

CHAPTER 1

# AUDIENCE ANALYSIS

*Analyse your Audience Carefully*

Analyse your audience carefully and then shape the contents of your speech to achieve your objective and to connect with your listeners. Your speech should be audience-centred, should enable audience comprehension, and should take into account audience comfort. First comes the audience and then the contents of the speech. The contents are influenced by the kind of audience you have, not the other way around. When you are invited to deliver a speech, you are given an audience that you cannot change, but you can mould the substance of your speech to meet the needs of the audience.

If your topic is 'Taxation in India', the contents of your speech will be shaped by your audience. The material will differ depending on the type of audience. If, for example, the audience consists mainly of trainees like articled clerks, the contents would address simple and basic matters. If the audience consists of finance directors, the contents would be more advanced and technical. If the audience is made up of foreign investors, the contents would be broader in scope, concentrating on policy matters. The topic of 'Taxation in India' remains the same, but the substance, and the level of detail and focus, will vary depending on your analysis of the type of audience for your speech.

## WHAT IS THE SCALE OF KNOWLEDGE OF THE AUDIENCE?

Clearly, an important aspect of audience analysis is knowing the level of familiarity your audience has with the subject. What does the audience know about the subject of your talk? This knowledge can prevent you from setting an unreasonable objective, or overly ambitious goal, for your speech. To achieve your aim of connecting with your audience effectively, you need to perform an audience analysis based on the audience's familiarity with the subject. This could be divided into three stages:

**Stage 1:** The audience is unaware of the issues under discussion.

**Stage 2:** The audience is aware of the issues.

**Stage 3:** The audience is informed about key points.

Assuming your audience is at Stage 1 when it is, in fact, at Stage 3 can lead you to making a speech on topics that are already known to the audience. You can embarrass yourself by telling the audience what they already know. I once attended a conference on accounting standards where the audience comprised senior accountants, yet one of the speakers delivered a speech as if the audience knew nothing about accounting standards. In this case, there was a clear mismatch between expectation and reality, resulting from the speaker's failure to properly analyse the audience's level of knowledge and expertise.

## PERSONAL EXAMPLE

I was invited in 1993 to be part of an official delegation from the Federation of Indian Chambers of Commerce and Industry (FICCI) to visit the United States to promote foreign direct investments in India (FICCI, United States, 1993). My subject was 'Taxation in India'.

My analysis of the speaking situation indicated the following unknowns:

- I did not know my audience in the United States.

- I did not know the organizers and co-sponsors.
- I did not know my co-speakers.
- I was not familiar with the locations where the speeches in the USA were to be made.
- My audience did not have any knowledge of me or the subject of my speech.

These unknowns required that I prepare my content and hone my delivery to address these issues for my presentations in the United States. I had to develop a separate game plan for this unknown audience. I had to do extensive visualization of my past successful speeches. I had to focus more and lay extra emphasis on certain techniques like stance and eye contact for achieving audience awareness. I had to personalize my speech with repeated references to the chairman, to the co-speakers, and to people in the audience. Additionally, I had to use more humour to reach out to, and connect with, my audience. Finally, I had to do hours and hours of rehearsals, practising much more than I usually do.

Contrast this with a situation where I am speaking on the same subject, 'Taxation in India', to a known audience as part of an in-house training programme in India. In this situation, I know the audience, I know the organizers, I know the co-speakers, I know the conference hall. Though the subject is the same, my ability to connect with my known audience in India, as compared to an unknown audience in the United States, is definitely greater.

The lesson this personal-speaking episode taught me was that where there are many unknowns in an equation, some of the techniques—these are discussed in this book—that you deploy need to be taken up many notches and applied in an enhanced and focused way. There is a clear correlation between the extent of the unknowns and the tactics you employ, both in terms of selection and emphasis. This requires you to work harder at:

- structure
- breaks and recaps

- eye contact
- stance
- personalization
- visualization
- practice

## ANOTHER PERSONAL EXAMPLE

I was commissioned to deliver a presentation on behalf of Birla VXL Limited at London (Birla VXL, London, UK, 1996) on the possibility of establishing a joint venture. I had to make out a case for why India and why a joint venture with Birla. I was the sole speaker. The presentation was to be made to a small group, in a room with a U-shaped seating arrangement. Again, the topic was new; the organizer was new; the audience was new; the location in a hotel in London was new.

To address these unknowns, I had to give greater emphasis to speech structure, breaks and recaps, eye contact, stance, body language, humour, and the closing summary. I had to back all this up with more visual aids, like supporting slides and handouts, and spend hours and hours on additional practice. I increased my rehearsals for the presentation enormously. I nearly doubled the hours of preparation that I would normally put in with a known audience at a known location. I started my practice in India. I continued the run-through of my draft speech at Hyde Park in London. I even did four dry runs in the presence of a small internal audience before the final presentation in London.

The lesson this personal-speaking episode taught me was the importance of audience analysis in determining the right techniques to be used in your speech and deciding where your emphasis needed to be.

## CONCLUSION

Your role as a speaker is to get as much information about your audience as you can, and to do this well before the actual day of the speech so you have ample time for doing a thorough audience analysis.

The two examples I have given above highlight the importance, first and foremost, of audience analysis. Ascertain how many unknowns there are in the equation and then proceed with your game plan. This may mean giving greater weightage than you would normally to certain techniques that will help in providing extra clarity like structure, breaks and recaps, personalization, flexibility, gestures, body language, visual aids, analogies, and humour, and putting in many more hours of rehearsals.

All this extra effort will be worth it, because if you can get the audience analysis right, you will be bang on target in connecting with your listeners.

# CHAPTER 2

# STRUCTURE

*Imagine a Series of Railway Wagons Coupled Together*

## HAVE A PROPER STRUCTURE

Every speech should have a proper path, a well-defined structure, and clear goals. It should have an opening, a main body, and a closing. In the main body, there should be a logical transition from one point to the next.

Think of the main section of the speech as a collection of modules or compartments, strung together like a series of railway wagons. Each wagon represents one main point of your speech. Four wagons represent four main points of your speech. Each module, compartment, or main point can be further divided into subpoints accompanied by supporting evidence like relevant details, examples, case studies, and facts and figures.

In keeping your main ideas in separate modules along with the supporting information, you have the option of shuffling these to suit the needs of your presentation, either prior to the speech or even while delivering the talk.

Organize your speech so that you have enough flexibility to move around some sections, paragraphs, or sentences (or even to omit them altogether) without sacrificing the major thrust should the occasion demand some adjustments to the text.

In delivering a speech, do not jump all over the place like the proverbial mountain goat. without a definite path or a clear plan.

Instead, ensure that there is a logical progression from the first wagon to the last wagon, with proper transitions between each wagon, or point. This simple organizing principle, then, is the foundation of speechmaking.

Essentially, as you move from one point to the next, tell your audience what you are doing and why you are doing it. Recap section number one, then move to section number two. Recap section number two, then move to section number three. Follow this sequence throughout the talk. An audience feels much more comfortable if they know at which stage they are in a presentation. After each section of your speech, allow enough time to recap the main points, as this summary not only helps to clarify the material but also reinforces the listener's sense of the structure of the entire presentation. Finally, before you end, tell the audience that you are about to end.

## DIFFERENT WAYS OF STRUCTURING YOUR SPEECH

You can employ various methods for revealing your main ideas to the audience. Here are some well-known ways of structuring and organizing your speech.

1. *Chronological* is the natural order of events, the recounting of events the way they occurred sequentially. For example, a person's life story would typically begin with childhood, proceed to adolescence and adulthood, covering important life events like graduation, marriage, children, career, and retirement, and end with old age and even death.
2. *The list* is the most common way of structuring a talk, calling for the points to be arranged in an arbitrary manner. This works best when there are only a few points, each of equal importance.
3. *Problem–cause–solution* is another method of structuring your speech. It works best when making a persuasive

argument, for example, in business presentations. This type of structure flows naturally from one point to the next and is therefore quite easy to follow.

4. *Thesis–antithesis–synthesis* creates audience interest and stimulates creative thinking and can be a powerful way of sequencing your presentation. In my speech on 'Why Accounting Standards?' (Association of U.K. Chartered Accountants, New Delhi, 1994), I used this thesis–antithesis–synthesis structure. For instance, in constructing a case for the adoption of International Accounting Standards, I began with a discussion of Indian Accounting Standards (thesis), moved to a description of the German Commercial Code (antithesis), and ended with an argument for International Accounting Standards (synthesis).
5. *Argument–counterargument* is a good way of laying out the points of agreement and disagreement on an issue. This is an effective way of dealing with the pros and cons of a proposal.
6. *Inductive reasoning* involves presenting facts that lead to a conclusion, or to the inference of a conclusion. It presents data and evidence leading to an apparently logical conclusion. This is well suited for a persuasive speech.
7. *Acronyms* offer another way of sequencing your presentation. Manjula Banerji, Partner, Deloitte, India, in a recent podcast titled 'Build Your Personal Brand', used acronyms brilliantly by structuring her speech on the 5 Cs: competence, commitment, confidence, communication, and cost-effectiveness.

## FINALLY

A speaker should know how to assemble ideas for a speech that will be interesting and engaging, with an orderly progression of thoughts supported by facts and examples. The speaker should know how to deal with the listener's distracted or wandering mind, and how to tackle the lack of motivation or interest on the part of the audience. To do this successfully, every speech should have a well-defined path and a proper structure. Your audience analysis, the size and nature of the audience, the physical venue, the time available, the facilities at hand, and so on, may influence your selection of the most suitable structuring method. Some sequencing methods are better than others. You should be prepared to test the effectiveness of one method against the other. Experiment with the different options available for structuring your speech and discover which ones are most effective in securing and sustaining audience interest.

# CHAPTER 3

## OPENINGS AND CLOSINGS

*Look at these as somewhat Akin to the Opening and Closing Ceremonies of the Olympic Games*

Many books on public speaking discuss the importance of proper openings and closings, often setting out at least ten ways in which to do so. This sometimes leads to contrived openings or closings, which may be a bit disjointed from the rest of the material, as the speaker hunts frantically for the best opening or closing.

I once attended a lecture by a visiting professor who, on arrival at the podium with an armful of books, contrived to lose control of them, so they toppled to the floor. Perhaps this deliberately staged mishap was his attention getter and opening, both combined into one action. However, it seemed rehearsed, rather than spontaneous.

### TYPES OF OPENINGS

While I do not wish to undermine the message conveyed by these books on public speaking, I can only share my own personal experiences in this matter. I let my openings emerge from my material. This may happen after many rehearsals of my speech, but definitely not immediately at the beginning of my preparation. I like to wait until I am deep into the construction of my speech before focusing on the right way to start. Additionally, my openings flow into my main sections fairly rapidly. I generally follow one of five main types of openings:

- headlines
- stories, examples, and illustrations
- quotations
- comparisons and analogies
- attention getters

## PERSONAL EXAMPLES

For example, if I am speaking on the subject of frauds, it is natural for me to refer to my own personal *story* of the Tri-Sure India Ltd fraud case and begin from there. Steve Jobs, a co-founder of Apple Computers, said, 'The most powerful person in the world is the storyteller.' Storytelling is the foundation of a good speech. Starting your speech with a story is a great way to hook the audience's attention.

When I spoke to audiences in the Unites States about investment opportunities in India (FICCI, United States, 1993) and the potential market offered by the burgeoning Indian middle class, in my opening remarks I made a *comparison* between the Indian middle-class population, estimated at 300 million, to the total population of the United States, estimated at 260 million. Always give comparisons to something that the audience can relate to. I made the size of the potential consumer market in India, as represented by the Indian middle class, meaningful by placing it in a certain context that American audiences could comprehend. Starting your speech with a comparison or analogy makes for a compelling beginning.

## ATTENTION GETTER AS AN OPENING BY KENNEDY

Many books on public speaking advise beginning with a bang—perhaps a witty observation, a pithy saying, a startling statistic, or a memorable statement—to catch the listeners' attention. This is an excellent suggestion, provided you can find an opening that is not obviously contrived. Kennedy, on an official visit to France, noting that his wife, Jacqueline Kennedy, was an instant hit and dazzling the French, decided to open his speech at a Paris press luncheon, to the delight of the French and American journalists, with these remarks: 'I do not think it altogether inappropriate to introduce myself to this audience. I am the man who accompanied Jacqueline Kennedy to Paris, and I have enjoyed it.' *What an attention getter!*

## HOW NOT TO BEGIN

Avoid opening your speech with the following trite phrases:

- Thank you so much, it's a pleasure to be here.
- I'm glad to be here.
- Thank you for that kind introduction.
- Thanks for coming.
- So, let's get started!
- My name is . . .
- I was only asked yesterday to give this speech.
- Will you please turn off your cell phones?
- I apologize for my voice.
- I'm not an expert, but . . .

## TYPES OF CLOSINGS

This final statement is the last chance for the speaker to influence the audience, or to drive home a message, so think through carefully at the planning stage about the exact words that you intend using. Note them on the prompt cards or memorize them. I generally say 'I am about to conclude' a few minutes before the end of my speech and before closing. Through this method I signal to the audience that I am nearing the end. I generally tend to follow one of the following five main types of closings:

- a summary of the main points
- the central message of the speech
- repetition of the opening as the closing
- attention getter
- question and answer session

I repeat the leading points mentioned in the main segments of my speech in a concise manner. In short, I summarize the principal points and give the audience something to take away with them. At times, I also restate the central message of the speech. Sometimes, I use my openings also as closings. Every so often, I use an attention getter to conclude my talk.

## QUESTION AND ANSWER SESSION JUST BEFORE CLOSING

Depending on the mood of the audience, I sometimes introduce an open question and answer (Q&A) session just before closing. This variation works well for me. Most speakers schedule the Q&A session after the speech, to be handled by the chairman of the session. Unless I am a part of a panel discussion, I, as the speaker, prefer to field the questions myself.

By holding the Q&A session just before your closing, you can often pick up some useful insights for your concluding remarks. In case there are any difficult questions, you can still control the final message after the Q&A session is over. You can downplay or ignore adverse comments or hostile remarks, if any, made during the Q&A session by re-emphasizing your main proposition more emphatically in your concluding remarks. In this way, you can end the talk positively, on your terms.

## FINALLY

After concluding your speech, return to your chair and sit down. Stop right there. Do not embellish your talk with added thoughts and last-minute observations. Do not let the speech end in an anti-climax. Do not thank the audience for listening. Do not apologize for anything. Do not make any more interventions. There should be no doubt in the mind of the audience that you have ended your speech.

## IN THE END

Clearly, every speech must have an opening and a closing. *Look at these as somewhat akin to the opening and closing ceremonies of the Olympic Games,* which are mass colourful rituals representing a celebration of sport. They employ the language of symbolism to communicate their message. Let it be so with the opening and closing of your speeches.

# CHAPTER 4

## BREAKS AND RECAPS

*Allow the Audience to Absorb Thoughts and Ideas by Incorporating Breaks and Recaps*

Resist the temptation to rush through your talk and finishing it as soon as possible. Hurrying from thought to thought, and from sentence to sentence, will prevent listeners from fully understanding the content of your speech.

It is vital that you allow enough time for the audience to absorb the information and insights you are presenting. You can do this by introducing breaks between thoughts, clauses, sentences, paragraphs, and segments.

As you move from one part of your speech to the next, stop for a short break. You do this by recapping, summarizing, or reiterating the previous thought. Have as many recaps as there are thoughts. If you have three segments in a speech, stop to recap the material three times. The recap forms the break between one segment and the next. It gives the audience a breather and a chance to digest the points made in the previous segment before moving on to the next segment.

### READING IS DIFFERENT FROM LISTENING

When you read printed text, you can flip the pages to reread a passage or to skip ahead. You can pause, take a break, and then start reading again. You can skim the material or engage in deep, intense reading. You can read silently or aloud. You have the freedom to select what you want to read, when you want to read, how long you want to read, and whether to read slowly or rapidly. You can underline passages and make notes and annotations in the margin.

Reading printed text enables 'dialogic reading'. This allows the reader to interact directly with the language and the content, and to absorb the material at a deeper and more meaningful level.

However, as part of an audience, listeners do not have all these advantages. Reading is different from listening. As a speaker, you can help listeners by summarizing and recapping the essential points of your talk, so that they know how far along the path you have progressed. In written form, these summaries and recaps may appear unnecessary and repetitive. But in speech form, listeners need these reiterations and reminders to help them follow your narrative as well as to help them retain what you are saying.

## PERSONAL EXAMPLE

In my talk on the subject of 'Frauds in India', at an event organized for a select group of managers and partners at Chennai (EY, India, 2020), I divided the speech into three parts:

- Is the justice system adequate?
- Is the whistle-blower policy adequate?
- What can the audit profession do?

Between each of the three segments, I gave a break and did a quick recap of my main points and arguments. After discussing the justice system in the first segment and before moving to the second segment, I said: 'I have indicated to all of you the need for reforms and revision in our justice system and the steps to be taken in this regard to prevent frauds .... Now I move to the next issue in my speech, that of the policy relating to whistle-blowers.' By doing this, I recapped the material I had just covered.

I guided my audience from one segment of my speech to the next segment. By building in smooth transitions and indicating the direction that I intended to take, I provided my audience a clear road map of my talk on the subject of frauds. In this manner, I added comprehensibility and clarity to the subject.

## TRANSITIONS

Breaks coupled with recaps serve to connect the different parts of your speech, providing both you and the audience essential memory aids and cognitive links. The comprehensibility and coherence of your speech depends on your skill and on the care you take in applying the connectors properly at the right places.

I generally like to use vocal or oral transitions, though you can also use visual or physical transitions. The best way of doing a vocal transition is to take a short break after finishing the first segment of your speech, pause, look at your prompt cards, and then continue. The break alerts your listeners that you are changing gears and transitioning to the next section in which you will discuss a new but related idea or proposition. The segue should be done smoothly, so that the audience is not disoriented or confused by a sudden switching between subjects or themes.

Another way to make a transition is to indicate it visually to the audience through a physical action. If you are speaking from a podium, move to the left or right of the podium as you speak your transition sentences. If there is no podium, move from one side to the other for your transition sentences. Even a shuffle will do. After speaking the transition sentences, you may move back to your original position. In this way, the audience can not only hear the transition from one thought to another, but also witness the accompanying and reinforcing physical movement.

Whichever transition method you use, make sure to rehearse the accompanying transitional movements carefully so that you can move smoothly from one segment to the next.

## CONCLUSION

Breaks and recaps act as transitions from one section of your talk to another section and provide the framework for a pleasurable listening experience. Listeners appreciate a proper structure to the presentation. A speaker who jumps all over the place like the proverbial mountain goat only confuses and frustrates listeners.

Mastering transitions is an important skill in your arsenal of oratorical techniques for making a powerful presentation. The judicious use of breaks and recaps can introduce order and clarity to your presentation, which will help your listeners follow the structure of the talk and grasp the content more easily. Breaks and recaps can enable a smoother, more memorable presentation and help make you into a more persuasive and powerful speaker.

## FINALLY

Here are two quotations on the importance of structure in a talk, accompanied by breaks and recaps.

Religious orators in the West often used a well-known tripartite template that emphasizes the power of repetition: 'Tell them what you're going to tell them; next, tell them; next, tell them what you told them.' This is a guaranteed way of hammering home the message.

Churchill said: 'If you have an important point to make, don't try to be subtle or clever. Use a pile driver. Hit the point once. Then come back and hit it again. Then hit it a third time—a tremendous whack.'

CHAPTER 5

# GATHERING THE MATERIAL

*Make Sure that you have Finished Speaking before your Audience has Finished Listening*

Limit the subject to three or four main ideas in a talk of forty-five minutes or less. If you attempt to cover too many points, your audience will lose interest. Initially, I fell into the trap of trying to cover too much material because I wanted to display my knowledge of the subject, but soon realized that a few main talking points supported by appropriate examples and illustrations is the perfect recipe for a successful talk.

Avoid packing too much information into your speech. Avoid showing off. Avoid burdening the audience with too many facts and figures, statistics and data, arguments and propositions. Avoid an excessive use of charts and graphs. Do not overwhelm your audience with an overload of information. Do not be content driven.

## LIMIT YOUR PRESENTATION TO THREE OR FOUR MAIN POINTS

1. *A few main ideas are better than a surfeit of information.* Dale Carnegie, the well-known writer, offers some valuable advice on public speaking: 'Develop reserve power. Assemble a hundred thoughts around your theme, then discard ninety.' From the balance, choose a few key themes

and relevant ideas, play around with them, and then cut this material even further. Detailed research on a chosen number of themes will help you deliver the final three or four thoughts with confidence and authority. Keep the remaining thoughts as reserve power in case you need to be flexible in your speech or when you have to address queries and comments during the question and answer (Q&A) session. Resist the temptation to show off, as the audience will quickly realize that your primary objective is self-promotion, not actual communication. An exposition of a few well-chosen ideas is better because the curated insights and selected analysis you offer are easier to remember not only for you but also for the audience.

2. *Factor in the audience's limited auditory processing.* The limited human capacity for auditory processing means that you should limit the speech to a reasonable amount of time and restrict the number of major points you address. Concentrating on a few major ideas and overarching themes is the best way forward. Structure your content into three or four areas, supported by examples, analogies, metaphors, picture words, and so on. Remember this dictum: rich in examples, illustrations, and stories; thin in facts, figures, and data.

3. *Prune the material.* When I prepare my presentation, I initially include many talking points, but after a few revisions and rehearsals I cut the draft drastically to a few points only. I return to my draft after a few days, when the first flush of creativity has died down, and I can see the script with a clearer, more dispassionate eye. This is pruning time when deadwood falls easiest to the axe. Yes, it is painful to cut ruthlessly, but that is the only way it will work. Limit your talk to a few carefully selected aspects, but add vivid, evocative details and interesting examples. I try not to do too much.

I try to follow the adage that less is more rather than adopt a *shotgun* approach that aims to cover eight to ten ideas. There is no way my audience will remember eight to ten main ideas. If I focus on three or four main ideas, I have a much better chance of ensuring that my audience will recall my message and what I had to say.

I try not to bury the audience under a barrage of facts, data, and slides. I try to go into greater depth with a few ideas rather than spreading more ideas around in a superficial fashion. Don't be afraid to cut even as much as half of your material; this will leave you with a text that is stronger, leaner, and clearer. Aim for a well-defined presentation with a sharp focus.

## TRANSFER THE MATERIAL TO PROMPT CARDS

I generally start with rough notes on A4 size paper. Then I edit and move the material from the A4 size paper to the first set of prompt cards, and thereafter to a series of prompt cards as required. I see these transitions as important because they help me refine my message. I practise repeatedly from each set of prompt cards and keep marking changes on them as I continue with my rehearsals. Even if my last set of prompt cards is cluttered with a lot of changes and crossings, I do not make a clean set just for my final delivery. I like to employ the last used set of prompt cards when I am delivering my speech.

If you were to examine my first rough notes on A4 size paper and the final prompt cards used by me for the last rounds of rehearsals, you will find that I have discarded a substantial part of the matter because it was repetitive, irrelevant, or excessive. It is better to cut the material drastically rather than keep it all and thereby risk leaving the audience confused about your message for lack of clarity and focus. Long speeches are dull and difficult to comprehend.

## FOLLOW THE 80/20 RULE

As you prepare your material, remember that most presentations fail because speakers try too hard to jam everything into their speech when, ideally, they should spend time rehearsing the presentation of the message. Speakers, early in their speaking career, seem to think that more content is better than less. Professional speakers know that delivery is critical, with less emphasis on material. Make sure to spend enough time preparing the delivery, undertaking as many rehearsals as necessary to reach fluency. Some speakers follow the 80/20 rule, meaning spending 80 per cent of time on rehearsing delivery and only 20 per cent of time on preparing the material. This distribution of time and effort may sound surprising, but it has proven to be highly effective for many speakers. Once you realize the worth of the 80/20 rule, you will embrace it too.

To gain fluency in the articulation of your speech, set aside sufficient time for practice. Do not accept a speaking engagement where your intention is to make an impactful presentation, but you are preoccupied and do not have the kind of time required for perfecting your speech. Remember the 80/20 rule, as this understanding is critical for extracting the most from the time and effort you expend in preparing your material. Spend less time in preparing and collecting your material, and much more time in perfecting your delivery.

## LINCOLN AND THE GETTYSBURG ADDRESS

Careful preparation sharpens your perception and gives you confidence. The more homework you do, the more spontaneous, confident, and relaxed you will be when you deliver the speech. Let the thinking process go on for a long time. Sleep on it; dream about it. Let the ideas sink into your subconscious.

Lincoln was known to mull over a speech for days, and even weeks. He carried small notes addressed to himself. Eventually he arranged these jottings in order and revised and edited these drafts into powerful speeches. He tweaked and polished his words right till the last minute.

The next time you are working on your speech, remember that Lincoln's famous Gettysburg Address in 1863 lasted two minutes and contained only 272 words. It is remembered as one of the most important speeches in American history and considered one of the best short speeches ever. It is said that the speech was finished before the photographer could even take a photograph of Lincoln. Edward Everett, the chief speaker at the dedication ceremony at the Gettysburg cemetery, clearly admired Lincoln's remarks and wrote to him the next day, 'I should be glad, if I could flatter myself that I came as near to the central idea of the occasion, in two hours, as you did in two minutes.' The power of words has rarely been given a more compelling demonstration.

## FINALLY

Franklin Delano Roosevelt, a former president of the United States, said: 'Be sincere; be brief; be seated.' Cut and chop your material, as Lincoln did with his Gettysburg Address. No one ever complains about a speech being too short. *Make sure that you have finished speaking before* your audience has finished listening.

# CHAPTER 6

# BACKBURNER

*Rehearsing by Day and Brewing Ideas by Night*

If I were to give a speech today, I can draw on more than fifty years of experiences and lessons learned, beginning in 1969 when I started my career. It is there in my brain, waiting to be unlocked.

I draw material for my speeches from my personal experiences and from books or the internet. It is a tremendous advantage today that many aspects of the topic of your speech can be researched online.

However, the core substance for my speeches comes from my personal experiences. I weave together facts and statistics with my personal experiences to prepare a speech. I cut and revise the collated material until I have the minimum necessary for a successful speech. The more chopping I can do, and the more material I can dump in the discard bin, the better.

## REHEARSING BY DAY AND BREWING IDEAS BY NIGHT

As soon as I have a workable draft, I prepare notes and start the first series of rehearsals. I let the material brew in my conscious mind. In the evening, I read my material once more before sleeping and then leave the further brewing for my unconscious mind as I sleep. I continue this process of *rehearsing by day and brewing ideas by night*. This often results in useful insights about how to arrange material or how to find the right opening for the speech.

A speech should have a firm foundation consisting of a good deal of subconscious thought that has already taken place. Ideas fall more readily into place when you give the matter your full attention, because a certain subconscious foundation has been laid.

## THE ANALOGY OF THE COOKING STOVE

Let's examine how we use the backburner of our stove. It is intended for the slow cooking of dishes we do not need to pay attention to right away, food that can wait a while. We relegate these dishes to the backburner while we focus on more urgently required dishes that we cook on the front burner. The slow cooking of ingredients on low heat over a period of time on the backburner results in a tasty dish, full of complex flavours and enticing aromas. Similarly, let your ideas simmer on the backburner of your mind on slow and gentle heat, allowing it to untangle knots, resolve difficulties, or address problem areas in your speech. Often this patient and unhurried treatment results in some useful guidance or understanding about how you should proceed with your speech.

The backburner does not only have to work while you sleep. Follow the same process of using your backburner during the day when you are engaged in some activity like gardening, cooking, cleaning, bathing, walking, or exercise. In principle, it means allowing your mind to solve a problem while you are doing something else.

One way of activating your subconscious mind is to ask it a question that triggers thought. Do this as you get ready for bed, thus priming your mind for action as you sleep. For example, you may ask: how should I begin my speech? Let your subconscious mind go to work for you. It will produce an answer, although it may take days. Be ready for possible awareness to come at any time.

## WOLFGANG AMADEUS MOZART

The Austrian music composer Wolfgang Amadeus Mozart (1756–1791) who profoundly shaped Western classical music claimed that he got the ideas for his operas and symphonies while travelling in carriages. He said: 'When I am, as it were, completely myself, entirely alone, and of good cheer—say travelling in a carriage, or walking after a good meal, or during the night when I cannot sleep—it is on such occasions that my ideas flow best, and most abundantly. Whence and how they come, I know not, nor can I force them.'

## THOMAS ALVA EDISON

Thomas Alva Edison (1847–1931), the inventor of the phonograph and the incandescent light bulb, set the stage for the modern electricity-driven world. Edison, possibly the most famous and tireless inventor in the United States, after working for long hours, often napped and found answers to problems with which he was wrestling. He said: 'Personally, I enjoy working about eighteen hours a day. Besides the short catnaps I take each day, I average about four to five hours of sleep per night.'

Edison used his famous catnaps to not only recharge his batteries; he also used his subconscious to work on solving creative problems. A working nap required sitting upright in a chair, making it harder for him to fall into a deep sleep. To further prevent himself from falling into deep sleep, Edison held a steel ball bearing in each hand and placed metal pie pans at his feet. After power napping for a while, he would relax sufficiently for the ball bearings to slip from his hands and fall into the pans, with the noise waking him up.

Edison hung onto consciousness while moving towards sleep to get the benefit of a sort of emotional and cognitive wandering of the half-awake mind.

These wanderings can be guided gently, as Edison did, or left open to roam freely wherever the mind wants to go. Guided wanderings have the benefit of keeping a topic of our interest in mind, so that we can observe it from new angles to learn new things. Edison meant business by creating conditions so he could stay in this state for long periods. These pleasant and fruitful wanderings through his mental landscape led to many of Edison's inventions.

## CONCLUSION

I am no Mozart or Edison, but the methods they followed in tapping into their subconscious mind are worthy of study. For me, my subconscious works best after I have done a few rehearsals with my prompt cards and have reached into the heart of the speech to the extent of about 50 per cent. I may even feed the backburner particular thoughts and ideas, facts and variables, and wait for all this to simmer overnight as I sleep.

I am often surprised by some useful insights thrown up by my unconscious mind, which ultimately find their way into the final draft of my speech. Suddenly, there is comprehension, perception, and cognizance, as though a light bulb has been switched on.

## FINALLY

Even in writing this book, I have sought the help of my backburner. For example, insights emerging from my backburner led me to give more prominence in the book to the Tri-Sure India Ltd fraud case; to include a chapter on yoga; to add a chapter on Lincoln, Churchill, and Hitler; and to write a chapter on how to face regulators and law courts. These chapters did not appear in the first draft, but were added in the subsequent drafts. The credit goes to my backburner.

# CHAPTER 7

## RESERVE POWER

*Assemble Many More Thoughts than you are Likely to Need*

Start building reserve power by considering the theme of your talk as soon as you have been handed the responsibility of making a speech. As you prepare your rough notes, jot down the points that you intend incorporating, assemble many more thoughts than you are likely to need, then discard some of these ideas as you hone and polish the text. Collect more information—data and statistics, facts and figures, examples and case studies—than you are likely to require. Consider the total amount of material you have amassed as a block of marble out of which you have to chisel out your speech, chipping away excessive, repetitive, and irrelevant material. Keep chiselling away until you are finally left with the core or essence of your speech. Sweep the leftover bits and pieces into the discard bin.

### ACTIVATE THE SUBCONSCIOUS MIND

Let your subconscious mind mull over the theme of your talk during this incubation period and you will be surprised at the insights that emerge. I find a good time for this subliminal thinking is just prior to sleeping. My mind intuitively starts to work on the facts, data, and stories that have preoccupied me during the day, and often comes up with excellent suggestions. In this half-awake state, I can often decide, without much conscious deliberation and effort, what material to keep in my speech and what information to exclude.

## BUILD RESERVE POWER

The items that you have discarded need not be permanently jettisoned. You may dip into this material as and when required. For instance, at the speaking occasion, you may find it necessary to discard your original example for some reason, and because you already have backup material at the ready, you will not be at a loss as to what to do. Reserve power is tremendously useful when fielding questions around your topic. If you have got into the habit of collecting extra material at the preparation stage, you will be in a much better position to handle all types of questions that may be thrown at you after the speech.

The items tossed into the discard bin can be pulled out later whenever the situation demands it. You will be in a position to act confidently because you have come prepared, backed up by extra material kept in reserve. Consider the discard bin as the residuary reserve power you need as a backup for any adjustments you may need to make on the spot in your speech. In speechmaking, you have to be flexible and adroit, ready to suddenly switch gears and change tack in response to unforeseen circumstances and unexpected situations. The greater the resources you have in reserve, the greater your flexibility and the greater your ability to negotiate your way out of a potentially tight spot.

## PERSONAL EXAMPLES

I remember that at the speeches I gave on 'Section 145 of the Income Tax Act, 1961' at an association of lawyers and advocates (Ghaziabad Tax Bar Association, Ghaziabad, 1997) and on 'Business in 2000 & Beyond' at a panel discussion (Management Development Institute, Gurugram, 1997), the Q&A sessions went off extremely well. This was because I had built plenty of reserve power, relying on information that I had collected but had never actually used in my speech.

In these Q&A sessions and panel discussions, I dipped into my residuary reserve power and pulled out extra material lying in my discard bin in order to handle the queries with self-assurance and confidence. The lesson for me from these two speeches was the need to build reserve power and to collect more material as a safety measure in order to remain flexible, mentally agile, and ready.

## FINALLY

*Assemble many more thoughts than you are likely to need.*

# CHAPTER 8

# PROMPT CARDS

*Mark the Prompt Cards with Keywords Only*

## READING A SPEECH IS NOT RECOMMENDED

Reading from a script has certain disadvantages because it prevents effective communication with the audience. If you read a speech, you lose authority, as your energy and attention are focused down towards the script lying on the podium, instead of radiating outwards towards the audience. You will appear as if you lack commitment and interest, even if that is not the case. It will be difficult for you to be aware of the audience, and their reaction, without making eye contact.

So, what is the alternative? Speaking from an outline is the recommended course of action. This will enliven the atmosphere, enabling you to establish eye contact and thereby connecting and interacting with the audience.

The outline can be in the form of notes. These notes should ideally contain your opening and closing statements, the heading of each module, and the main points. They should contain reminders about where you want to smile, pause, break, and recap. They should indicate the points in the speech where you want to show a visual aid. They should include your picture words and keywords. But your notes should not include your speech word for word.

## WHY PROMPT CARDS WORK FOR ME

Depending on your preference, you can make your notes on a legal pad, normal stationery, or index cards. I prefer using index cards or *prompt cards*, though I have also used normal stationery of various sizes from time to time.

Prompt cards enable you to refer to the main points of your speech, serving as cues during delivery. The cards are not meant to be read aloud to the audience, but are intended only to act as cues for you, the speaker.

Why do I use prompt cards? Because they are convenient. Because they help make me look prepared and polished. Because they encourage me to think on my feet.

## HOW TO USE PROMPT CARDS

- Use 4" × 6" cards.
- Use bullet points.
- Write only on one side of the cards.
- Use large capital letters and leave ample space between the lines.
- Mark the cards with keywords that only trigger your memory, acting as cues. Less is better.
- With experience you will be able to reduce the number of words on the cards. One word will act as a trigger for an entire section of your talk.
- Add an appropriate heading showing which part of the speech the card covers.
- Indicate the opening and closing of your speech.
- Write or print clearly using a larger than usual font size (so you can read the words easily, even from a distance, even in poor light).

- Mark the cards with colours and symbols (that is, colour code the cards), indicating instructions or cues for the display of visual aids, pause, rhetorical question, pace, voice inflection, and so on.
- Number the cards clearly on the upper right-hand corner.
- Do not staple the cards together. Keep them separate and loose.
- Practise with the cards so that you are familiar with the trigger words and markings on them.
- Use the same cards that you have used for practice rather than preparing a final fresh set for the talk.
- When speaking, quickly glance at the card, then look up and convey your thoughts from memory and in your own words.
- Slide the cards to the left (on the podium) as you finish with each one, leaving only two cards upturned at any one time.
- When you finish your speech, the cards should be in a neat pile on the left side of the podium, with the first card at the bottom.
- Do not shuffle or play with the cards as you speak.
- If you are running short of time, you can quickly summarize the contents of some cards or omit some other cards.
- If you are well under the time allotted to you, you can add more cards.
- The cards fit easily into the inner pocket of your suit or jacket or dress. They are small, light, unobtrusive, and highly portable.

## THE ADVANTAGES OF PROMPT CARDS

- You will sound natural and relaxed because you will be choosing your own words as you speak.

- You will be confident because you will have a safety net.
- You will establish eye contact with the audience because you will not be reading a speech and will not have to keep looking at your papers.
- You will be able to use expressive body language because you will be free to move as you please.

## FINALLY

Mark approximate timings on the prompt cards so you can track your progress through your allotted time. If you find you are going over, you can make an adjustment by leaving out an example or two. Conversely, if you are under time, you can add a card.

You are now ready to get going. All you need is a packet of standard prompt cards, a selection of highlighters, and a good pen with a distinctive ink (red, green, purple, or any other bright colour) that can be read easily. Try using prompt cards in your next speech and see how you like it.

# CHAPTER 9

## PRACTICE

*Nothing can be Created from Nothing*

Rehearsal is a critical step in the preparation for powerful speaking. It is essential to *practise, practise, practise* at every opportunity.

Stand in a room familiar to you, or in your garden, with your prompt cards and run through your speech, addressing an imaginary audience, and using all the techniques of effective public speaking described in this book.

A technique that works well for me is improvising a stage in a room. I stand in front of a high table, using it as a podium. As I run through my speech, I glance at various items of furniture, using chairs, books, lamps, flower vases, ashtrays, and bric-a-brac to serve as members of a mock audience. I also stand in my garden and rehearse, pretending that various bushes and shrubs are my audience.

### IDENTIFY THE PLACES WHERE YOU STUMBLED

Go through your speech many times, glancing at your prompt cards as you proceed. At the beginning, you will be hesitant and lack fluency. But don't worry; try and run through your entire speech without stopping. Make a mental note about the places where you stumbled or lacked fluency. You will be tempted, particularly at the rough spots, to stop and consult your notes, but resist this. It is essential that you finish your practice session in one go, come what may.

After you have run through the speech once, go through the places where you stumbled and then concentrate on improving these weak areas in separate rehearsal sessions. When you are ready for your second practice session, go through the speech from start to finish. Continue this process until you feel that you have reached a satisfactory level in terms of articulation, enunciation, pacing, and so on. At each rehearsal, repeat the entire speech. After a few run-throughs, you will find that your stumbling points are getting fewer and fewer. After many rehearsals, you will be able to achieve fluency and smooth delivery.

## DO NOT MEMORIZE WORDS

Do not memorize the text of your speech, but instead familiarize yourself with the main talking points so thoroughly that you are able to speak in an extemporaneous manner, using your notes as a guide. Practise until you are 100 per cent confident. Practise in different settings and at different times, testing different presentation techniques. Practise while playing golf or tennis or any other sport. Practise in front of a mirror while taping your performance with a voice recorder or a video recorder. Practise in front of close friends or relatives or people whose judgement you trust. Diversify your practice sessions in various ways to motivate yourself.

## PRACTISE WHILE PLAYING GOLF

Another effective way of rehearsing is to go over your speech while doing something else, like cooking, gardening, walking, or playing a sport. Many years ago, I used to polish my speeches while playing golf. The theory here is that you try and reach fluency in your delivery while doing another task when your mind is preoccupied. By bringing in a diversion as you practise your speech, you are training your mind to remember ideas and themes in a distracting environment. Surely, on D-Day when you actually deliver your speech with full concentration, you should be at an advantage because you have already rehearsed your delivery while only half concentrating or being otherwise distracted. Try this method. It worked for me. My golf may have suffered, but my speech on D-Day hopefully did not.

## PRACTISE WHILE PLAYING TENNIS

Tennis players can polish their speeches while lobbing balls and smashing shots on the court. By speaking (silently, of course) and moving around at the same time, you can train yourself to talk in spite of distractions. Multitasking will help improve your ability to focus on more than one thing at a time. If you are able to train yourself to speak despite distractions, imagine how easy it will be for you to speak on the actual day, without distractions. You can accomplish this feat if you simulate a distracting environment as you rehearse your speech.

## PERSONAL RHYTHM AND FLUENCY

How many times should you run through your speech? This is a matter of personal choice. You have to decide when you have attained the desirable personal rhythm and fluency. Initial rehearsals may lead you to make changes to your prompt cards, adding or deleting sections, or moving around material. Generally, I find that I need at least *twelve* rehearsals from the date my prompt cards are fully ready, except for minor changes. This is the minimum number of practice sessions I need to reach a certain rhythm and a comfortable level of fluency.

You should rehearse repeatedly until the thoughts and themes of your talk are ingrained in your mind so firmly that your speech appears natural and effortless. On D-Day, you are then free to speak from your heart in an authentic manner.

## PERSONAL EXAMPLES

For example, for my presentation on 'Tax deducted at source' (Logic Consultants, New Delhi, 1998), I could only put in three dry runs. I immediately realized after my presentation that my speech lacked proper articulation, eloquence, rhythm, and fluency. I often hesitated and got stuck, searching for the right words and trying to marshal my thoughts. My insufficient preparation had resulted in a less than satisfactory speech.

Another example of inadequate preparation was my presentation to the Clal Group (Birla VXL, Tel Aviv, Israel, 1997). Here I spent the bulk of my time sight-seeing and exploring a city I had not visited before, at the cost of proper rehearsals. Once again, my rhythm and fluency were not satisfactory. I also failed to understand the effect of my presentation being scheduled towards the end of the visit, after all the factory visits and other discussions had been concluded. Ideally, to make an impact, my presentation should have taken place at the beginning of the visit to the country. I should have identified this scheduling problem at the audience-analysis stage and then taken suitable steps to address it.

However, each failure is an opportunity to learn and to resolve to do better the next time.

## CONCLUSION

To recap, if you want to give a memorable presentation:

- Practise, practise, practise.
- Practise your speech without a break.
- Practise silently or loudly, as you prefer.

- Practise while you are getting ready for work.
- Practise while you drive to work.
- Practise while you play golf or tennis or any other sport.
- Practise at least a dozen times.

## FINALLY

Delivery is the final step to eloquence. It requires practice and discipline, and you can be your own personal trainer. Speaking well is not just a matter of chance or talent. Unless you sweat it out through hours of solid relentless practice, nothing will come of it. *Nothing can be created from nothing*. As Dale Carnegie rightly observed: 'Only the prepared speaker deserves to be confident.' It is best not to accept an invitation to speak if you do not have the discipline or the time required for proper preparation and rehearsal. Dry runs are essential for successful presentations. Public speaking is an art which only improves with repetition. Lincoln summed it up best: 'If I had eight hours to chop down a tree, I'd spend six hours sharpening my axe.'

CHAPTER 10

# RECORDING

*Share your Results with a Speech Counsellor or Experienced Speaker for Feedback*

## STUDY YOUR VOICE

An effective method of rehearsing is to record your speech and then play back the recording so you can analyse it carefully to identify weaknesses. Once you have found your vulnerabilities, you can concentrate on improving your performance.

You can use a voice recorder, mobile phone, laptop, or other suitable device to record yourself making a speech. During the height of my speaking career, I used the older-generation Sony IC. Through a memory stick voice editor, I transferred my recorded speech from the Sony IC to my desktop computer. I could then sit back, relax, and listen to my voice through the computer speakers, searching for the highlights or low points of my speech.

Look for pause, phrasing, diction, articulation, voice modulation, and so on. Make notes about the areas where you need to improve. Pay particular attention to the pace of your delivery and check whether it is too fast or too slow. In the beginning, it may be better if you look for only one defect, say, monotony of pace. Keep a copy of your draft speech or draft notes in front of you and tick the places where this trait is most noticeable. Play the recording repeatedly to catch other defects or weaknesses. You may discover a lot of things that you may not like, perhaps a vocal mannerism that you were not aware of and would like to eliminate. After a few 'dummy' runs through the revised script, rerecord the corrected version of the speech and notice the difference. In this manner, you will be in a position to transform an indifferent or pedestrian speech into something more memorable and impactful.

I am not suggesting that you do this for all your speeches, but trying it out selectively for, say, every fifth speech will do wonders for your overall presentation skills. If you can do it more often, all the better.

## EXAMINE YOUR STYLE OF DELIVERY

A video recording of yourself speaking allows you to see what the audience sees. It allows you to spot the most glaring errors in your style and delivery, and troubleshoot these problems quickly and easily.

Delivery includes elements like eye contact, stance, choreography, smile, gestures, and body language. You may find that you are indulging in far too much head movement or nodding, gesticulation, frowning, and pacing. You may not be making effective eye contact, you may be slurring your words, or adopting a poor stance.

Alternately, there may be mannerisms that are annoying to the audience. Try to identify and then eliminate these distracting behavioural tics by going over the recording of the speech numerous times.

**Here are some things you need to look for in the self-video:**

- eye contact
- hand gestures
- stance
- pacing
- rate of speaking—quickly or slowly

- volume of speech
- pauses
- enthusiasm
- facial expressions
- confidence
- transitions
- choreography

## FINALLY

Voice record yourself. Video record yourself. Watch the recordings and carefully study your performance. Identify your strengths and weaknesses. Highlight areas that need improvement, gaps that need to be filled, places where you need to add transitions. Compare these recordings with videos of your earlier performances so that you can learn and continue improving.

Send the recordings and your own self-analysis of your performance to a speech counsellor or experienced speaker for feedback. Then incorporate the suggestions and recommendations made by these experts. You will notice improvements in your speaking style, stance, delivery, and overall presentation skills.

# CHAPTER 11

# EXERCISES

*Do these Exercises to Improve your Performance*

Plenty of information is available on the internet on exercises for improving diction, so I will not cover them in detail here, except a few taken from my personal diary of speeches which I have maintained for many years.

These are exclusive exercises that I have built into my daily schedule and that I do by rotation. You can do these exercises over a period of time or selectively as a quick fix on the day of the speech to boost your confidence and to release tension.

## BREATHING

The power, resonance, and depth of a voice depend almost entirely on how breathing is regulated. As the ability to control the breath increases, so does the capacity to adapt the breath to the needs of speech making.

Pay special attention to the role of the diaphragm in the control of breathing. Try to strengthen the diaphragm so that you can increase your breathing capacity and lung power, thus reducing the need to stop to catch your breath in between phrases or sentences. Since the power and resonance of your voice emanates from your diaphragm or stomach, it is worth spending time on doing stomach-strengthening exercises regularly.

## SOME BREATHING EXERCISES

- Stand with your feet shoulder-length apart. Inhale deeply and hold your breath. Pull the stomach muscles in and pump in and out as many times as possible, all the while holding your breath.
- Inhale deeply and begin counting aloud while holding your breath. Aim to count till thirty in the beginning. As you become more adept at this counting exercise and increase your breath control, try counting to a higher number and to extend your voice to the far corners of the room and even beyond.
- This exercise is designed to give you a sense of how much breath you need for expressing thoughts of varying lengths. Inhale deeply and then as you exhale say:

  'sh' seven times in one breath<br>
  'sh' three times in one breath<br>
  'sh' as one long sustained sound
- Take a short breath and exhale slowly through your mouth, expelling your breath through your teeth in a fine thin stream, like a hiss. You should be able to silently count to thirty the first time and then to seventy with more practice.
- Pretend your index finger is a candle. Hold it 10 inches away from your face. Direct your breath at it in a thin stream. Now hold your finger 18 inches away and aim your exhaled breath at it.
- Inhale deeply and then try saying this sentence smoothly all in one breath without pausing: 'One of the tests of leadership is the ability to recognize a problem before it becomes an emergency.'

## ARTICULATION

Articulation is a form of oral or verbal gymnastics involving the tip of the tongue, the teeth, and the lips. Our lips, teeth, tongue, throat, and jaw all contribute to clear diction and articulation.

You can loosen the tongue and facial muscles by doing regular tongue and face exercises a few days before your speech. Stick the tongue out to the left, to the right, and then straight out as far as it will stretch. Stretch it in and out for a few minutes. Make sure to do these exercises regularly, and particularly in the days before the speech. This will help improve your articulation and diction.

## SOME ARTICULATION EXERCISES

Repeat the letters:

- www www www www
  bbb bbb bbb bbb
  wbn wbn wbn wbn
- p p p p
  pp pp pp pp
  ppp ppp ppp ppp
  pppp pppp pppp pppp
- a e i o u
- lld ddd lll ddd
  *ldl ldl ldl ldl*

Repeat the words rapidly:

- lah-rah lah-rah lah-rah
- We have rubber baby buggy bumpers.
- Peter Prangle picked prickly prangly pears.
- In Tooting, two tutors astute tried to toot to a duke on a flute
  but duets are gruelling, end only in duelling, when tutors astute toot the flute.

Try the kiss-and-smile exercise:

- say 'oo' as in 'toot'; then 'ee' as in 'deed' in quick succession ten times

## POWER STRETCHING

Practise power posing by extending your arms and hands out sideways or overhead as far as they will go and then holding this position while you continue breathing. This power stretching is similar to some yoga asanas. This boosts confidence and energy, and eliminates nervousness and stress.

## SHAKING THE EXTREMITIES

Shake all your extremities or limbs (legs and arms) vigorously. Move your head around and lift and flex your shoulders to loosen things up.

## BENDING AT THE WAIST

Bend over at the waist, letting your neck and arms hang loosely. Then come up slowly, vertebra by vertebra. When you are erect, say with confidence: 'I am ready.'

## FIGHTING ANXIETY THROUGH EXERCISE

If you experience anxiety, nervousness, stress, or apprehension before or during your speech, you can overcome (or at least reduce) these feelings through exercise or physical activity. Make sure you enjoy the benefits of physical exertion and exercise—running, cycling, yoga, working out in the gym, golf, tennis, or any other sport you enjoy—in the days leading up to the speaking event and particularly on the morning of the talk. Exercise releases endorphins, naturally occurring chemicals in our body that relieve pain or stress and increase happiness and a sense of well-being. All you need to give a good speech is to feel confident and calm.

## SPEECH RATE

How fast do you speak? A common response to anxiety about public speaking is to race through your speech, getting faster and faster until the words are flying out of your mouth and are incomprehensible to the audience. The best cure for fast speaking is to record your speech and then play it back. Then work to correct the defect.

## PRACTISING IN FRONT OF A MIRROR

Practising in front of a mirror will help you to actually see how you deliver your speech. It will allow you to identify and correct any annoying mannerism or other defect or weakness you may detect. Once you have identified your stance, gestures, and body language, you can decide which one to develop and keep and which one to discard.

## FINALLY

All of these exercises require a long-term investment in time and effort to improve your performance in public speaking. On the day of the speech, you can allot at least thirty minutes in the morning to do some or all of these exercises. They will make you a better and more confident public speaker.

# CHAPTER 12

# VISUALIZATION

*Desensitize Yourself through Creative Visualization*

## RECALL YOUR PAST SPEECHES

Before making your speech, recall the many successful speeches you have already given. The recollection should be of your favourite experiences. Recall speeches where you were enthusiastic and positive. Recall speeches that ended well and brought you applause, smiles, congratulations. Recall speeches that resulted in many congratulations sent by email. Recall speeches that led to coverage in newsletters or the press. Recall the events in detail. Retrieve these recollections of past successes from your memory and get into the habit of reliving them mentally. The more you activate these images, the more force they will have.

## VISUALIZE THE CURRENT SPEECH

Now visualize the current speech that you are about to deliver. Visualize yourself entering the conference hall. Visualize yourself meeting some of the organizers and members of the audience with warmth, interest, and enthusiasm. Visualize your name being announced as the next speaker. Visualize yourself getting up and walking to the podium. Visualize yourself making a successful delivery. Visualize prolonged applause. Try to do this visualization exercise every day for a week before the event. Do it definitely as you drive to the speaking event.

This is known as the power of visualization. In all my speaking events, I employ creative visualization to gain confidence and to prepare myself for the big day. I envision myself being totally in control—smiling and laughing, gracious and charming, warm and friendly, enthusiastic and energetic. Visualization definitely helps me in delivering a better speaking performance. With practice and repetition, confidence and ease become natural attributes, and visualization is a powerful tool for gaining this self-assurance.

## VISUALIZE AS NEAR AS POSSIBLE TO THE REALITY

Your simulation could be based on your knowledge of the speaking situation, location, venue, conference hall, timing, names of organizers, and names of co-speakers. Try to simulate the situation in your mind's eye as near as possible to the reality. Of course, there will be many unknowns, so you will have to fill in some details based on your experience about what to expect. Even if you have to guess the unknowns, try to fill in the details in a realistic manner. If you have made a speech before at the exact location, it will help in the simulation or visualization. If not, visit the venue before the actual event, if possible, to get a feel of the conference hall.

The advantage of creative visualization is that on the actual day of your speech, you will feel you are already in a familiar zone, because you have already simulated it often in your mind. Familiarity breeds comfort and makes it easier for you to cope with the actual presentation. *Desensitize yourself through creative visualization.*

## WASIM AKRAM AND HIS INSWINGERS

Many successful sportspersons use the visualization technique to create a vivid image in their mind of the desired outcome. They visualize their performance before the actual performance, thus increasing their chances of delivering a better performance. Top cricketers visualize their success in taking a critical wicket or scoring the winning run. They make visualization a daily activity to go alongside their regular cricket practice.

For example, Wasim Akram, the well-known fast bowler from Pakistan, has said that he used to visualize most of the deliveries that he bowled. If there was a reverse swing, he would bowl three away swingers and then the inswinger. But before he bowled the inswinger, he would vis ualize it and would see (in his mind's eye) the ball swinging from outside the off stump into the batsman's pads or hitting the stumps.

## HOW TO DESENSITIZE YOURSELF

You can follow certain techniques to desensitize yourself to any apprehensions you may be harbouring about the speaking event.

Here is one technique. Imagine a thermometer. The bottom of the thermometer is your position of least anxiety (0) and the top of the thermometer is your position of most anxiety (100). Think of an anxiety ladder, starting with the lowest anxiety threat and ending with the highest anxiety threat. Work from the bottom up as follows:

***Step 10:*** Delivering the speech

***Step 9:*** Sitting at the podium

***Step 8:*** Arriving at the venue

***Step 7:*** Doing relaxation exercises on D-Day

***Step 6:*** Waking up on D-Day

***Step 5:*** Practising on the day before the speech

***Step 4:*** Rehearsing the speech at home

***Step 3:*** Preparing the material for the speech

***Step 2:*** Learning that you have been invited to give a speech

***Step 1:*** Sitting at home reading a book

You can use this anxiety ladder to desensitize yourself. Relax and close your eyes and imagine the lowest level of threat. Now work your way up the ladder, imagining the threats at each level. Visualize the threat at each level and allow yourself to experience it for some seconds. Work on metaphorically climbing the anxiety ladder at least two or three times a day.

You will notice that as you do this visualization exercise repeatedly each day, your apprehension levels will start decreasing. Eventually you will arrive at a point where you will stop worrying about your imminent speech. Your initial nervousness about the speaking event will be replaced with confidence and ease. This is the power of systematic desensitization, a tried and tested technique for improving performance.

## CONCLUSION

Systematically planning how you will approach your speaking engagement days in advance of the event, and then overcoming your anxiety step by step through visualization, are essential tools for successful speeches. The desensitization technique recommends that we imagine ourselves performing certain activities successfully a number of times, and consequently build up expectation of mastery at the actual performance.

Whenever I have applied this technique of creative visualization, I have arrived at the speaking event feeling that I am already in a familiar zone. I have visualized the event so many times in my mind that on D-Day it does not lead to any panic or sudden uneasiness. It works for me and it will work for you.

CHAPTER 13

# VISUAL AID

*Visual Aids should be used only to Reinforce the Main Points*

Speech-making is not exclusively an oral process and can be greatly aided by visual aids. Visual aids can amplify the speaker's message by summarizing the main talking points and thus help the speaker connect with the audience.

The danger lies in relying on visual aids as a substitute for the actual presentation. Often the visual aids take over and the speaker assumes a secondary or even redundant role. It is important for the speaker to maintain full control over the visual aids, using them sparingly and judiciously.

If visual aids are treated as adjuncts or supplements to the communication, and not the communication itself, they can have a considerable impact. They should be used only to reinforce the main points—to aid the process of communication, and not to take it over completely. They may be grouped together or spaced out over the course of the talk, depending on where you need to reinforce or clarify your message.

## TYPES OF VISUAL AIDS

Visual aids encompass props and displays, white boards, flip charts, printed material like handouts, leaflets, and booklets, overhead transparencies, pre-prepared glass-mounted slides, PowerPoint decks, photographs, and videos.

The choice of visual aid is primarily determined by the audience size and the configuration of the conference hall. White boards and flip charts may be suitable for small audiences, whereas a PowerPoint (PP) deck is better for larger audiences. Overhead transparencies and slides may be more suitable for small and medium-size audiences, where dimming the lights is not an issue. I have made presentations using the following visual aids:

- *White boards.* I used these for staff training programmes.
- *Flip charts.* I used these for staff training programmes.
- *Handouts and booklets.* I used these at the residential course at Kufri, near Shimla, organized by the Northern India Regional Council of the Institute of Chartered Accountants of India (NIRC, Kufri, 1989); at a presentation to the trustees of WWF-India (WWF-India, New Delhi, 1996); and at other conferences.
- *Overheads: transparencies* made in advance. These can be used in a brightly lit room, so you can maintain eye contact with the audience. This was my preferred method for staff conferences.
- *Overheads: pre-prepared glass-mounted slides* operated through a carousel slide-tray. These have to be sourced and pre-prepared by a third party and once made cannot be changed. This can be a disadvantage. Establishing eye contact can be a challenge as the room requires dimmed lights for effective viewing. I used these for my presentations for Birla VXL (Birla VXL, London, UK, 1996; Tel Aviv, Israel, 1997).
- *Microsoft PowerPoint.* I find this the most convenient option, because you can make changes on your laptop right until the start of your speech. You can transfer the final presentation from your laptop to a pen drive, which is then inserted into the common laptop being used at

the conference. I have used PP presentations for partners' conferences (Deloitte, India Partners' Conferences, 2004, 2005, 2006).

- *Videos and photographs.* These are more recent innovations and can be powerful visual tools.

## CONCLUSION

I like to mix different types of visuals in my talks for diversity. For instance, I mix handouts with overhead transparencies, or combine slides with handouts and booklets. I follow the minimalist approach in preparing PP decks, firmly believing in the dictum that less is more. I like to begin my slide presentation with minimum information, and then add 'pop-ups' to fill the empty spaces while I discuss each subpoint.

Make sure that the visual aids you employ are clearly visible to the entire audience. Make sure that you talk to the audience and not the visuals. Make sure that when you have finished your talk, the visual aid is removed or turned off.

# CHAPTER 14

# POWERPOINT PRESENTATIONS

*Do not let the Slides Take Over the Communication*

PowerPoint (PP) presentations have become ubiquitous in our times, and the usual method of formulating presentations, particularly business presentations.

## DO NOT LET THE SLIDES TAKE OVER THE COMMUNICATION

As an independent director on the boards and committees of various companies, I have had to endure many hours of PP presentations. I often wondered how much more productive and interesting the speaker would be if he simply took control of the talk, relegating the slides to a secondary, even subservient, role.

The slides are often packed with so much information that they are neither readable nor comprehensible. Speakers seem to think that the more text and bullet points they can manage to cram into a slide, the better and more impressive is their presentation. They follow the mantra 'more is better', rather than 'less is better'.

Gradually, the speaker loses control, yielding the floor to the PP presentation. As the barrage of slides continues, the speaker seems to disappear into the background. Soon the audience too loses interest, as they cannot digest all this information coming at them relentlessly through slide after slide.

I submit to speakers that they would be much more effective if they used the slides to support their main points and not the other way around. I tell them not to let PP take over. Many PP presentations mostly shift the focus away from the speaker to the slides, and the speaker consequently loses control and fails to make eye contact with the audience, which are essential elements for successful public speaking. If you want to establish a personal connection with the audience, make sure to minimize the use of slides and also reduce the material they contain. Slides crammed with excessive information detract from the main message. *The slides should not take over the communication.* Do not let this happen.

## THE AUDIENCE CANNOT MULTITASK

We cannot listen attentively to the speaker and simultaneously look at and read the text on the slides in any meaningful manner. Our eyes shift constantly from the speaker to the text on the slides as the speaker presents slide after slide. It is difficult, if not impossible, for us to pay attention to multiple inputs. We cannot multitask. Our brains are incapable of processing inputs simultaneously from two different sources—text from the slides and words from the speaker—in a coherent way. We cannot absorb and digest this information being thrown at us. This cognitive dissonance, or clash in understanding, can be reduced or even eliminated if the speaker uses as few slides as possible, and that too only as a supportive or supplemental aid to the narrative provided orally by the speaker.

## PERSONALLY

I am not particularly thrilled at having to use PP in my presentations. On the contrary, I enjoy the challenge of getting my message across without PP. It compels me to use all the strategies discussed in this book—storytelling, anecdotes, pause, phrase, humour, and rhetorical devices—most effectively. If I succeed without the use of PP, the greater is my satisfaction.

If I do have to use PP, for me the minimalist approach works best. I use my slides as a backdrop to my message, and not as a replacement. I like to start with the minimum material and use 'pop-ups' as I go along to supplement my message. I usually add the relevant material on the slides point by point as I speak.

The author of a book on public speaking describes the perils of an overreliance on PP. He arrived at a business conference and when his turn to speak came, he announced, 'I have to apologize for not coming prepared with a PowerPoint presentation for you.' The audience cheered and applauded widely, as all the five preceding talks had been well-rehearsed PP presentations. The audience was thrilled at not having to endure another PP presentation.

## LESS IS MORE

Some speakers rely on PP presentations in an ill-advised attempt to impress the audience with detailed data, knowledge, and analysis. But as a tool of communication, the PP presentation is inferior and far less effective than a speaker who employs stories, analogies, picture words, quotations, pauses, phrases, and rhetorical devices, and uses less data and fewer bullet points in PP slides. Speaking directly to the audience—without using PP or other visual aid as a crutch—is a more compelling form of communication.

Let us remember the words of the English poet and playwright Robert Browning in his 1855 poem *Andrea del Sarto*: 'Less is more.' The phrase is often associated with the German-born American architect and designer Ludwig Mies van der Rohe (1886–1969) who championed simplicity and clarity in style. Write down this useful advice and follow it the next time you are preparing PP slides.

## CONCLUSION

I am not against visual aids provided they are used judiciously and sparingly to supplement the speaker's message. Communicate your ideas verbally as best you can, and use slides, charts, photographs, or videos to reinforce your ideas. If you cite statistics or data, present one major data point on one slide after you have conveyed the message verbally. Do not clutter the slide with too much information. Keep it simple and direct. Audience retention is thereby enhanced.

This has implications for the designing of slides. Do remember that humans are incapable of reading and comprehending text on a screen and listening to a speaker at the same time in any meaningful manner. Hence, do not stuff the PP presentation with an overload of information and data, nor try to dazzle the audience with technical wizardry. What we need is for people to speak in a humane, personal way that touches our hearts and inspires us to action.

# CHAPTER 15

## STORIES

*Think of the Ethos, Logos, and Pathos Content of your Speech*

### DALE CARNEGIE

I am not a born orator. I developed some ability because I wanted to teach myself the skill of public speaking, and so became my own coach. One of the first books I read when I was a young professional was Dale Carnegie's *How to Develop Self-Confidence and Influence People by Public Speaking*. I bought a copy in October 1983 and still go through it even today. My copy is heavily marked with my underlines and comments made many decades ago. This was the first book that taught me the single most important aspect of public speaking, which is to speak through stories. I was deeply struck by Carnegie's observation: 'The average speech would be far more appealing if it were rich and replete with human interest stories.'

### CARMINE GALLO

Decades later, Carmine Gallo echoed Carnegie's insights on public speaking in his 2014 book *Talk Like TED: The 9 Public Speaking Secrets of the World's Top Minds*. Gallo has an entire chapter on the subject, 'Master the Art of Storytelling'. He writes: 'Stories illustrate, illuminate and inspire.' Carnegie's first book on public speaking was published in 1926, so the two books are separated by eighty-eight years and yet both emphasize the art of storytelling as one of the main secrets of successful speaking. Gallo writes: 'Carnegie based his advice on intuition, but today we have brain scans to prove Carnegie right.'

## STORIES HOLD OUR ATTENTION

Based on my personal experience of delivering speeches for more than forty years, I can confidently state that using compelling stories in your speeches will hold the attention of listeners. Offer your audience a rich brew of stories. Stories and narratives stimulate and engage people in a way that dry facts and cold statistics cannot, making it much more likely that listeners will agree with the point of view of the speaker. They help to overcome audience disinterest and break down resistance.

## INSPIRATIONAL STORIES

Good storytelling is not a God-given gift or innate ability. Good storytellers master their craft through conscious effort and years of practice. Stories can be personal accounts of incidents that have happened in your own life or they can be narratives about other people; in both cases, the stories are inspirational and motivational, instructive and educational. Inspirational stories from your personal life are often sure winners, because they are sincere, authentic, and genuine. The audience will warm up to you even more if you share something about yourself and reveal your own feelings, vulnerabilities, and weaknesses. Never underestimate the power of the past and the impact of a few self-revealing incidents and episodes that have deeply influenced you or changed the trajectory of your life.

## PERSONAL EXAMPLE OF THE TRI-SURE INDIA LTD FRAUD CASE

More recently, in a speech on 'Frauds in India', organized for a select group of managers and partners at Chennai (EY, India, 2020), I narrated my personal story of the Tri-Sure India Ltd fraud case to illustrate the auditor's position on the detection of frauds. I described how I had to appear as a witness on behalf of A.F. Ferguson & Co., the defendants in the suit filed against it for its alleged failure to detect the fraud and how the firm was eventually acquitted.

I discussed how this case illustrates that an audit cannot discover all types of fraud. The system of internal controls can be corrupted and circumvented through the collusive efforts of the management. Collusion by the top management to commit fraud that usually involves sophisticated schemes, forgery, and misrepresentation is nearly impossible to detect unless information is provided by a whistleblower or if there is something strange or alarming that arouses the suspicion of the auditor.

The details of the Tri-Sure India Ltd fraud case, as available in the public domain and on the internet, indicate that this case had all the necessary elements of a fraud: misrepresentation; duplicate sets of documents; bogus 'mother' invoices; bogus delivery challans, gate passes, transfer slips, and costing records; secret and hidden godowns; a transport carrier who was part of the conspiracy; some customers who were 'hand in glove' with the management; and even an admission by the officer in charge of the accounts that he had falsified the auditors' initials and markings.

The fraud was disclosed by a whistleblower, Mr Singaravelu, head of the purchase department of the company, to an independent director of the company, Charles Grundy of Little & Co. It involved the manipulation of accounts and the role of secret and hidden godowns.

I was present at Santa Cruz airport in Bombay (later Mumbai) to meet Mr Wheaton, a director of the parent company, as soon as he arrived from the United States. Together with other company directors, we proceeded to the hidden godowns where stocks had been secreted. As I narrated this personal story in my speech, I was definite and specific. I offered details and names.

## DIG DEEP INTO PERSONAL EXPERIENCES TO FIND STORIES

I look at it like this. I have had a rich and successful professional life for nearly fifty years and now in my retirement I am busy with nature and wildlife conservation. Over the years, I have accumulated many stories, anecdotes, and personal experiences that my audiences might find interesting and entertaining, perhaps even instructive. Why not share them with my audiences? All of us have stories worthy of recounting to others. Examine your own life experiences and you will no doubt find a relevant experience that you can use in your next speech to illustrate an important point.

Some speakers are reluctant to talk about personal experiences because they think this may be too trivial or too restrictive. I hold the opposite view. I believe that if you talk about what life has taught you, and do so honestly and candidly, you will gain many devoted listeners. But this does involve digging deep into your bucket of personal life experiences and a willingness to share the lessons you have learned along the way. Believe me, if you do this sincerely, you will be much more effective, entertaining, and moving in your speech.

## ETHOS (CREDIBILITY), LOGOS (LOGIC), AND PATHOS (EMOTION)

Facts and figures, data and statistics alone are not enough to connect with your audience. An emotional connection through storytelling is far more helpful in getting your audience to understand and appreciate your point of view. Aristotle, the Greek philosopher and master of rhetoric, said that the art of persuasion is based on ethos (credibility), logos (logic), and pathos (emotion). Ethos represents the credibility, integrity, and trustworthiness of the speaker. Lagos represents the information, data, and logic presented by the speaker. Pathos represents the emotional content of the speech or the storytelling ability of the speaker.

In my speech making, I use at least 70 per cent of pathos (emotion) through examples and illustrations (basically storytelling) to get my message across. This template has stood me in good stead. Why should I change my blueprint when my personal experiences have helped me establish a rapport with my audience?

The next time you give a talk, *think of the ethos, logos, and pathos content of your speech.* If you find that you are not getting through to your audience, change the mix to perhaps 60 per cent of pathos and see the results. If you still fail to connect with your audience, change the mix to 70 per cent of pathos by including more stories, examples, illustrations, and anecdotes. I can guarantee that as you increase the pathos (emotional) content of your speeches, you will succeed in forging a much stronger bond with your audience.

## LINCOLN AND HIS STORIES

Lincoln came from a humble background and eventually became one of the greatest presidents in the history of the United States, from 1860 to 1865. He was a great storyteller and a master in using stories, anecdotes, illustrations, metaphors, analogies, colloquial expressions, symbols, and imagery to influence and persuade his audience. Lincoln said: 'I have found in the course of a long experience that common people—and, repeating it—common people, take (stories) as they run, are the most easily influenced and informed through the medium of a broad illustration than in any other way.'

## CONCLUSION

Audiences find it easier to remember compelling stories. Stories fulfil a primary need of human beings—the desire to know what happens next. If you can blend the art of storytelling with some of the other strategies described in this book (like pause, phrase, voice inflection, and rhetorical devices), you will have an unbeatable combination that will impress your audience with a memorable listening experience.

Grab the audience's attention by using people's names if this is not offensive to the individuals involved. Introduce the element of human interest. Use evocative language and unusual turns of phrases. Do not be abstract or vague. Do not talk in generalities. Be specific and concrete.

## FINALLY

If you are a busy person, with a packed schedule, and if you have time to read only one chapter in this book, I recommend that you read this chapter, 'Stories'.

CHAPTER 16

# SPECIFICS

*Build a Speech like a Layer Cake of Examples and Illustrations*

## EXAMPLES AND ILLUSTRATIONS

A good speaker makes only a few well-chosen points, limits the number of ideas presented, and backs up each argument with supporting evidence. From the beginning, compel your audience to sit up and listen by offering concrete evidence and specific examples.

If there is one technique that I regard as the gold standard for effective public speaking, it is the art of building a speech like a *layer cake of examples and illustrations*. This method calls for the inclusion of specifics, like examples and illustrations, and the exclusion of abstractions and generalities. A speech is far more appealing and memorable if it offers specifics like real-life examples and case studies, personal stories and anecdotes, quotations and analogies, and facts and figures, at times supported by visual aids.

The richest source of human-interest stories is your own experience and background. Weave your personal stories and unique experiences into the speech as real-life examples. This is the surest way of holding the attention of an audience. Back up every major point with examples and illustrations. Remember this sequence: major point, example, major point, example.

Be specific, definite, and concrete. The audience will then listen more attentively. Your speech should be full of words and phrases that conjure up images in the minds of listeners and make them see things from your point of view. This method of persuasive speech making, which relies on concrete case studies, distinctive examples, and evocative stories, will be remembered long after the talk is over. In contrast, an abstract, vague, ill-defined, meandering, unfocused speech will be boring and monotonous, and hence eminently forgettable. The very purpose of speaking would then be defeated, as the cardinal rule of speaking is never to be dull.

## PERSONAL EXAMPLE

Let me give you an instance of the power of the example. I was in the United States as part of a delegation led by the Federation of Indian Chambers of Commerce and Industry (FICCI) to talk about India's economic liberalization in 1991 (FICCI, United States, 1993). To explain liberalization, I gave a specific real-life example of Modi Xerox Ltd, a joint venture between the B.K. Modi Group and Rank Xerox Ltd, UK, established in India in 1983, to manufacture photocopying machines during the licence-quota raj.

I explained the opening up of the Indian economy through the example of this joint venture. I described how under the industrial licence given to this company, many significant aspects of doing business were regulated by the government. The company had no say and was expected to follow the dictates of the government as laid down in the industrial licence:

- the exact location of the project
- the number of physical units of photocopying machines to be produced
- the number of units to be exported
- the value of the imports

I further elucidated that under the liberalized scheme, the licence-quota raj system had been done away with completely, and that all the rules and restrictions that had existed in the pre-reform years would no longer apply when it came to doing business in India. In other words, henceforth there would be no restrictions of the kind that had existed under the licence-quota raj and that Modi Xerox Ltd had had to endure. Rather than talking in abstract terms and generalities, I was specific and explained the far-reaching impact of the economic liberalization of 1991 through the example of a particular joint venture.

Nearly two years later, I met Dr Amit Mitra, one of the delegates and the chairman of my session, who shortly thereafter became Secretary General, FICCI, and subsequently the finance minister of West Bengal. He actually remembered, word for word, the Modi Xerox Ltd illustration given by me to explain the changes in India's industrial policy to American audiences in 1993. If ever I needed an affirmation of my speaking style, this was it.

The impact of this specific illustration taught me the value of using real-life examples to support and explain my point. I did not use PowerPoint presentations or any visuals and yet I was able to connect with the audiences in the United States through the adroit use of this example. I made sure to always include case studies, illustrations, and precedents in all my speeches thereafter. The true example is the finest way of making an idea clear, interesting, and persuasive.

## ANOTHER PERSONAL EXAMPLE

During a discussion in 2020 with J.M. Seth, Senior Partner, A.F. Ferguson & Co. and Deloitte, India, while I was writing this particular chapter, he vividly remembered the example of G.E., India that I had given in one of my lectures on determining sample sizes for audit verification many years ago. It was the specific reference to G.E., India that had stuck in his memory despite the passage of more than twenty years since the lecture. Such is the power of a well-chosen example to make your point. A well-researched argument can be enhanced by an appropriate illustration from real life. It is not only the research on the topic that is essential but also the manner of delivery through the careful selection of the right kinds of examples (specifics). Very often, novice speakers do the research but forget the equally important matter of ensuring the effective delivery of the material through the inclusion of salient examples. Specifics are remembered, abstract concepts are not.

## NANI PALKHIVALA

Listening to the eminent jurist Nani Palkhivala, particularly on the government's annual budget, was a rewarding lesson in public speaking because he made liberal use of examples and illustrations in his analysis. That is why he was a highly sought-after speaker, particularly on the annual budget, attracting the largest audiences in the country. He spoke simply and directly, in language that the audience could understand, employing stories and anecdotes. For him to be abstract was anathema.

## OTHER SPECIFICS

In addition to examples, illustrations, and stories, here are some other types of specifics that you can present. All these are covered in greater detail in various chapters of this book.

1. *Personalization and dialogue.* At an annual partners' conference (Deloitte, India Partners' Conference, Mumbai, 2004), I noticed that many foreign delegates were more actively involved in the proceedings than I had anticipated. Keeping this in mind, I changed gears during my presentation in the afternoon and started interacting with them from the podium much more than I had originally intended. With some delegates, I *personalized* my talk by referring to them by name, like Peter Bowie, Frank Kolhatkar, and Terry Noble. With some others, I

entered into a *dialogue* from the podium on a one-to-one basis. I improvised. I was flexible. I went with the flow and adapted my presentation to suit the needs of the audience.

In my talks, I have often used dialogue to connect with the audience. I engage in a dialogue with a fellow speaker or panelist, or have an interaction with a member of the audience. This direct engagement makes you sound like a real person, someone who is approachable and affable, and helps to dramatize your talk. You may pick a person already known to you from the audience and carry on a dialogue with him. You may set this up beforehand, but being impromptu is more fun. Nothing prevents you from having a mini question and answer session in the middle of your speech in order to explain a major point. This kind of variation, embodying flexibility and spontaneity, in your speech style will always generate audience interest and engagement.

2. *Comparisons and analogies.* In my speech on 'Frauds in India' to a select audience of about fifty managers and partners at Chennai (EY, India, 2020), I compared frauds to a migraine headache. Frauds can never be totally eliminated, but can only be controlled, just like a migraine. As I suffer from migraines, I know that there is no cure for this affliction, but many drugs can help reduce the frequency and intensity of some headaches. You can also get migraines less often when you avoid the triggers that cause them, such as sitting directly in the sun or being in crowded areas. By comparing frauds to a migraine, I was better able to explain a complex subject in terms that the audience would easily grasp.

   Comparisons between the known and the unknown, between the familiar and the alien, help the audience grasp difficult concepts. Comparisons include similes and metaphors also. Charles de Gaulle, a former president of

France, used a simile to make a political comment: 'Treaties are like roses and young girls. They last while they last.' The American writer Truman Capote used a perfect simile to describe the enchanting city of Venice, Italy: 'Venice is like eating an entire box of chocolate liqueurs in one go.' Comparisons and analogies enable you to point out similarities between two different things. Employ these excellent rhetorical techniques to explain topics that may be too complex to describe in a short speech.

3. *Quotations.* In my farewell speech at my last annual partners' conference (Deloitte, India Partners' Conference, Goa, 2007), I paraphrased a quotation from *In the Arena: A Memoir of Victory, Defeat, and Renewal,* a book by Richard M. Nixon, a former president of the United States. Towards the end of my speech, I said that during my career of thirty-nine years as a chartered accountant, I had been on the 'highest mountain and in the deepest valley'.

   Use quotations that are relevant and appropriate. They can help lighten the moment and encapsulate your thoughts most effectively. Do your homework and search for suitable third-party quotations either online or in books. You can always find something fitting in the speeches and writings of personalities like Lincoln, Churchill, Kennedy, Martin Luther King, Jr., Mahatma Gandhi, Jawaharlal Nehru, George Bernard Shaw, and Shakespeare.

4. *Facts, data, and statistics.* Most presentations can usually be enhanced by backing up the main ideas with facts, data, and statistics. Make sure that all your information is taken from reliable and unimpeachable sources. Do not rely on hearsay facts and figures. Make sure that the numbers you cite in support of your claims are meaningful and understandable by placing them in a context that the audience can relate to. Use graphics to help clarify numerical data. Round off big numbers. Interpret statistics

by translating them into human terms. Make comparisons interesting by juxtaposing unusual and unexpected elements.

In 2020, I saw a video of a speech by an African leader, Prof. P.L.O. Lumumba, in which he described the economies of the African states as 'Mickey Mouse' economies. He compared the GDP of Ghana as being possibly equivalent to one-third the GDP of the city of Beijing in China; the economy of Burundi, worth two billion US dollars, as being the same amount as that earned by an American professional boxer in one year; and the economy of Benin as being smaller than the annual advertising budget of Coca-Cola. The speaker compared the GDPs and the economies of certain African countries by making interesting *comparisons* to things that the audience could relate to. He made the numbers meaningful by placing them in a context that any audience could understand.

5. *Visuals.* Choose from a variety of suitable visuals and illustrated matter like handouts and booklets; charts and graphs; photographs and videos; and props and displays. Mix them up for variety. In the presentation on behalf of Birla VXL at London (Birla VXL, London, UK, 1996), I used many slides to support my talk on 'Why India?' and 'Why Birla?' I also used handouts and a printed booklet at the end. I chose a combination of slides, handouts, and printed brochures for this presentation to bolster my message.

## CONCLUSION

Any speaker would like it said of his speech that it was interesting, memorable, powerful, and engaging. Abstract concepts are difficult for listeners to process. An oral narrative based on the emotional content of a story or an example or illustration is a far more effective way of connecting with an audience. The surest way of doing this is to use examples and illustrations, piling them up as in a layer cake, supported by other devices like personalization, dialogue, comparison, analogy, quotation, facts and data, visuals, all of them presented in a meaningful manner.

CHAPTER 17

# A VARIETY OF TECHNIQUES

*Multisensory Experiences add Interest and Variation to your Talk*

A powerful and memorable speech includes a variety of techniques that provide multisensory experiences and thus keeps the audience engaged and attentive.

Multisensory means tapping into the five senses of sight, sound, touch, taste, and smell. The senses of touch, taste, and smell are not often used in speeches. If you include techniques focusing on sight (visual) and sound (auditory), the two main senses that are relevant for speeches, you are more likely to connect with your audience and make the desired impact.

## EXAMPLES OF TECHNIQUES THAT STIMULATE THE VISUAL AND AUDITORY SENSES

Visual (the sense of sight)

- examples, illustrations, and stories
- photos, videos, and animations
- smile
- stance
- body language
- gestures

- handing out documents or brochures
- inviting a member of the audience to the podium
- engaging in a dialogue with a member of the audience
- choreography
- word pictures
- metaphors and analogies
- antithesis
- rhetorical devices

Auditory (the sense of sound)

- voice modulation and inflection
- pace
- pause
- phrase

## PROVIDING VARIETY THROUGH MULTISENSORY TECHNIQUES

Multisensory experiences are vital for creating variation and for ensuring audience interest in a speech. Make presentations that include techniques that stimulate more than one of the five senses of sight, sound, touch, taste, and smell.

The use of diverse methods piques audience interest and encourages listeners to stay focused on your message. Monotony kills audience interest. If you include compelling stories, stirring images, and evocative picture words in your presentation, it will be impossible for your audience to be bored. Voice modulation and inflection help in emphasizing important points, adding dramatic flair and enhancing your speaking style.

Scientific studies show that the inclusion of a visual model (stimulating the sense of sight) and an auditory model (stimulating the sense of sound) are key factors in forging strong connections with an audience. Leave science aside, I can vouch that with a variety of techniques in my presentations, I have been able to connect with my audiences in an effective and meaningful manner.

Appealing to and stimulating the audience's visual and auditory senses is the key. Reading out a speech will get you nowhere because your presentation will be remembered for being lackluster, tedious, monotonous, and dull.

## INCORPORATING MULTISENSORY TECHNIQUES

When I am asked to make a speech, at the design stage itself, I try to include as many multisensory techniques as possible so as to create a diversity of experiences for the audience.

I make a special effort to incorporate variety in my presentation.

I make sure to include stories, quotations, metaphors, variation in voice, picture-creating words, photos, videos, and rhetorical devices. I mark places in my prompt cards where I need to pay special attention to body language like establishing eye contact and adopting a balanced stance.

Of course, it is not possible to include all items that create diversity in a speech, but if you are aware of the importance of including at least some techniques, and if you can plan for this accordingly, you can be assured that your presentation is likely to be successful.

## MULTIPLE COMBINATIONS OF MULTISENSORY TECHNIQUES

You can combine stories and examples; incorporate photos, videos, and PowerPoint slides; adopt voice modulation and pauses; employ rhetorical devices; and engage in choreography. These elements can be combined in various ways to achieve the maximum impact. Combine and mix these multisensory techniques as you like. Give your audience a multisensory experience and they will remember your speech.

Include in your speech a visual model of the *sense of sight* in multiple combinations to enhance the listening experience. For example, focus on stories, anecdotes, smile, stance, choreography, gestures, visuals, word pictures, and metaphors to evoke a variety of sights or images in the mind of the audience.

Include in your speech an auditory model of the *sense of sound* in multiple combinations to enhance the listening experience. For example, focus on articulation, tone, cadence, volume, pace, phrase, and pause to give your audience a variety of sound-based or aural experiences.

## TEN STRATEGIES FOR YOUR NEXT SPEECH

In your next speech, include the following ten strategies to heighten the impact of the senses of sight and sound, and see the results for yourself. These audiovisual elements will make your speech much more interesting and compelling. These strategies are described in more detail elsewhere in this book.

1. *Distributing handouts or reading aloud from documents.* At a presentation to an audience of about forty people at a residential course at Kufri, near Shimla, organized by the Northern India Regional Council of the Institute of Chartered Accountants of India (NIRC, Kufri, 1989), I created diversity and interest. In the middle of my presentation, I asked people sitting in the front rows to hand out some documents to other members of the audience. I then asked the audience to read the documents.

   During my speech on 'Frauds in India' to a group of select managers and partners at Chennai (EY, India, 2020), I requested Suresh Subramanian, the chairman of my session, to read out a relevant passage from a document on the top ten accounting scandals in the past decades, which I had downloaded from the internet and printed out. This created diversity and audience involvement.

2. *Inviting a member of the audience to the podium.* On two occasions at annual partners' conferences (Deloitte, India Partners' Conferences, Mumbai, 2004 and Mumbai, 2005), I requested two partners, S.R. Tata and Jaideep Bhargava respectively, to come up to the podium and elaborate a particular technical point for a few minutes.

   Of course, you must inform the person in advance of your intention and give a stipulated time of a few minutes only. The person you have selected should not leak out his anticipated role in advance to the audience, as the element of surprise is essential in this technique. It goes without saying that the chosen individual should prepare his message in advance under your instructions, so that both his message and your message are in harmony. This technique should be used sparingly, perhaps only once in a presentation.

   I often follow this method while chairing the meetings of audit committees. I sometimes request an invitee to the audit committee meeting to elaborate on a particular point or to explain an issue in more detail. This is an effective method for emphasizing an important issue that you want the audience to remember.

3. *Choreography.* Another technique is to change your speaking position. At an annual partners' conference (Deloitte, India Partners' Conference, Mumbai, 2005), I moved from a standing position to a sitting position and then back to the standing position behind the podium. The audience is more likely to remember a relevant point made by the speaker when he is seated. Adopt different stances and positions so that your presence on stage is dynamic. This will allow you to connect with your audience and be remembered.

   Another way to appear dynamic (or at least, not static) is to shuffle to one side and make an important point from the side of the podium. Of course, you must have space to move; don't fall off the stage. But such digressions from the podium must be few and far apart, perhaps once or twice during the presentation. The basic principle is to stand behind the podium for most of the time and step away from it only once or twice, particularly when you wish to emphasize a particular point. Choreography is usually preplanned, but may also be impromptu if the urge arises and the moment is opportune.

4. *Visuals.* Include relevant photos and videos in your presentation. Laptops make the use of multimedia presentations and slideshows highly convenient. It is well established that images are far more likely to be remembered and recalled than words.
5. *Rhetorical question.* Try asking a rhetorical question in your speech for effect. Here is an example from Ronald Reagan, former president of the United States, at the 1980 Republican National Convention, delivering his acceptance speech as the party's presidential candidate. In this speech, Reagan used a series of rhetorical questions, referred to as *stacked* rhetorical questions, to criticize the presidency of his predecessor and opponent, Jimmy Carter, the presidential candidate of the Democratic Party:

   Can anyone look at the record of this Administration and say, "Well done"? Can anyone compare the state of our economy when the Carter Administration took office with where we are today and say, "Keep up the good work"? Can anyone look at our reduced standing in the world today and say, "Let's have four more years of this"?
6. *Antithesis.* Antithesis is widely used in speeches. In this famous example, the American boxer Mohammad Ali describes his tactics against his rival in the match that was billed as the Rumble in the Jungle in 1974: 'Float like

a butterfly, sting like a bee—his hands can't hit what his eyes can't see.' Here Mohammad Ali brilliantly contrasts two animal actions: a silent (floating) butterfly and an aggressive (stinging) bee.

7. *Analogy.* In a speech on 'Frauds in India' to a select group of managers and partners at Chennai (EY, India, 2020), I used an analogy to describe frauds. To emphasize that frauds can never be eliminated completely no matter how hard we try, I likened frauds to a plant called lantana, widely found throughout forests in India. Lantana is considered a noxious weed and is difficult to eradicate. Animals avoid it because it has thorns. By comparing frauds to lantana, I was able to convey to my audience the attributes and nature of frauds in a meaningful way. I was able to provide a context that the audience could relate to and understand. I am certain that many of my other abstract words will be forgotten with time, but not my analogy comparing frauds to lantana.
8. *Pace.* Vary the pace or tempo of your speech to hold the attention of your audience. A faster pace is usually associated with a narration, story, or illustration. A slower pace is usually associated with important passages and serious messages, which are spoken more softly, deliberately, and solemnly.
9. *Downward inflection.* Another technique is to introduce cadence in your vocal tone. Cadence means the rhythmic flow of sound in general. One aspect of cadence is a downward inflection of the voice, particularly when making an important point or at the end of a declarative sentence. Downward inflection, the slight falling in the pitch of the voice, adds authority to your words.
10. *Pause.* Introduce a pause to create variation and interest in the delivery of your speech. Pause before making an

important point or pause after making an important point; either way is acceptable. Try it and see the effect. However, do not employ a pause more than once or twice in a speech, otherwise it will lose its effect. The pause imparts authority and gravitas, and generates audience awareness.

## FINALLY

The nineteenth-century American poet and philosopher Ralph Waldo Emerson said: 'Speech is power: speech is to persuade, to convert, to compel.' If you fail to incorporate multisensory experiences in your talk, you will be categorized as a dull and boring speaker. If you give your audience a multitude of multisensory experiences, you are more likely to deliver a speech that is powerful, persuasive, and compelling.

CHAPTER 18

# MEMORABLE MOMENTS

*These will add Sparkle and Interest to your Speech*

Based on my experience of public speaking, I can confidently say that the inclusion of one thing that is memorable and vivid often makes an emotional impact, captures the attention of the audience, reinforces the main themes of your speech, and is long remembered after the event. It could be a story or anecdote, an example or illustration, a rhetorical device or declamatory technique, a word or phrase.

Excellent examples are Churchill's use of the memorable words, 'I have nothing to offer but blood, toil, tears and sweat' and Kennedy's inspiring exhortation, 'And so, my fellow Americans: ask not what your country can do for you—ask what you can do for your country.'

## HERE ARE SOME MEMORABLE WORDS, PHRASES, AND PROVERBS FROM HISTORY

- *Duty, honor, country*, General Douglas MacArthur
- *Read my lips: no new taxes*, George W. Bush
- *The silent majority*, Richard M. Nixon
- *Ich bin ein Berliner*, John F. Kennedy
- *Old soldiers never die*, General Douglas MacArthur
- *Senator, I served with Jack Kennedy, I knew Jack Kennedy,*

*Jack Kenney was a friend of mine. Senator, you are no Jack Kennedy*, Lloyd Bentsen

- *The Iron Curtain*, Winston Churchill
- *The cult of the individual*, Nikita Khrushchev
- *The only thing we have to fear is fear itself*, Franklin Delano Roosevelt
- *I have a dream*, Martin Luther King, Jr.
- *Give me liberty or give me death*, Patrick Henry
- *All power tends to corrupt; absolute power corrupts absolutely*, Lord Acton
- *To be or not to be, that is the question, Hamlet*, William Shakespeare
- *All that lives must die, Hamlet*, William Shakespeare
- *He who cannot smile ought not to keep a shop*, Chinese proverb
- *Even the lion has to defend himself against flies*, German proverb

## PERSONAL EXAMPLES

At an annual partners' conference (Deloitte, India Partners' Conference, Mumbai, 2004), I gave the audience a memorable moment. This was when I paid tribute to a partner from the Canadian member firm, Yezdi Pavri, who had played an instrumental role in finalizing the MoU and in enabling A.F. Ferguson & Co. to become a member firm of Deloitte. I called on the audience to applaud Mr Pavri, a gesture that was deeply appreciated, particularly by the foreign delegates present, as no one else at the conference had mentioned his significant contribution, let alone asked for public recognition or sought applause for him.

In a recent speech at the farewell to Shobinder Duggal, the Finance Director of Nestlé, India Ltd (Nestlé, Gurugram, 2020),

I ended by requesting the audience of company directors and senior executives to stand and applaud Shobinder who had had an outstanding career of many decades with the company and deserved every bit of the accolade. This was a memorable moment. Over the course of my long association with Nestlé, first as the statutory auditor and finally as a member of the board and as chairman of the audit committee, I had come to know Shobinder very well and admired his many fine qualities, financial acumen and expertise, and professionalism. This was one speech I relished making. When you speak from the heart, the task is easy, and indeed a pleasure.

## CONCLUSION

In your next speech, include memorable words, phrases, and proverbs, and incorporate moments that add some sparkle and interest. These should arise naturally and spontaneously, and should not be forced or contrived. They should be genuine and pertinent in the context of the speech. Try to include at least one memorable moment in your speech. It could be a word or phrase, a personal story or reminiscence, a photograph or video. It could involve calling up to the stage a member of the audience, or applauding a person in the audience, or asking the audience to do something, or having a surprise guest. Whatever you do, make sure it is relevant and appropriate to the occasion. Give the audience something special and unique, so they will be talking about it for days afterwards.

CHAPTER 19

# CONFERENCE HALLS

*Visit the Conference Hall before the Speaking Event if Possible*

A visit to the conference hall before the event will help you make any last-minute adjustments to your speech and speaking style. You will be able to see the layout of the venue, the placement of the speaking platform and podium, and the facilities available.

## DEALING WITH DISTURBANCES, DISTRACTIONS, AND INTRUSIONS

Once I arrived to give a speech at a small town and found that everything was wrong with the set-up. The lunch tables were arranged alongside an open conference hall, so that the speeches were constantly being disrupted by the noise of crockery being moved and the preparations for lunch. The doors of the conference hall were left open, allowing latecomers to stroll in at their convenience, creating a disturbance and distracting the speakers as well as the audience. This was a nightmare situation for any speaker.

For an optimal speaking arrangement, the conference hall should be closed once the speeches begin, with no entry allowed for late arrivals. Refreshments (tea, coffee, snacks) and meals should be served in a separate hall.

Even at important conferences, arrangements are sometimes haphazard and the atmosphere is casual. It amazes me that the typical arrangement at many speaking occasions is for the speaker to sit on the dais with the chairman and other co-speakers. Documents are handed to the chairman on the dais when the speaker is speaking. People on the dais shuffle their papers, whisper amongst themselves, fidget and yawn, omit to switch off their mobile phones, or even take a call on their phones. Large or ungainly props placed at awkward angles often obstruct the audience's view of the stage. Sometimes even a large bouquet of flowers can impede the view.

All this is disturbing to the audience and equally disruptive for the speaker. The speaker has to struggle that much harder against these distractions to keep the audience focused on his speech.

## SOLO SPEAKER ON STAGE: AN IDEAL ARRANGEMENT

Ideally, only the speaker should be on the stage, with no one else in attendance and no one hovering in the background. This eliminates any distraction caused by the movement of others on the dais.

When I arrive at a speaking event and find that I will not be sharing the platform with any other person, I heave a sigh of relief and silently thank the organizers. As a speaker, you are often not in a position to influence the arrangements, particularly if you are not hosting the conference. However, you can always let the host know in advance about your basic requirements, particularly if you are the keynote speaker or the only speaker.

## KENNEDY VS NIXON: THE FIRST DEBATE (1960)

The first-ever televised presidential debate in US history took place between Kennedy and Nixon on 26 September 1960, in Chicago, and was broadcast on CBS to 66.4 million TVs across the country.

It revealed the true power of television and simultaneously the critical importance of slick presentation. Kennedy's telegenic image and attractive appearance ensured a public relations victory for him.

Kennedy insisted on meeting beforehand with the producer of the debate who was managing the event, to check the design of the set and the placement of cameras. This was the kind of detailed preparation that he and his team did. As a result, Kennedy wore a dark blue suit that cut down on the glare of the studio lights and contrasted well with the grey studio background of the set, whereas Nixon's grey suit seemed to blend into the set and made him look wan and ill. Kennedy credited his performance in the first debate for his eventually winning the presidential election. He was already familiar with the studio setting of the first debate with Nixon and his performance was the better for it.

Similarly, the earnest speaker seeking to improve should visit the conference hall before the event to gain familiarity with the venue, and his performance will be the better for it.

## PERSONAL EXAMPLE

Knowledge of the setting helps you in visualizing yourself delivering your speech. It thereby instils confidence and helps you in performing more effectively.

If you are not familiar with the conference hall, visit it before the event if possible, as this removes one of the unknowns in making a speech. When I make speeches in places other than my home city, I try to visit the venue beforehand if convenient or arrive early at the event so I can familiarize myself with the conference hall and other arrangements.

For the six speeches that I gave as a member of the delegation from the Federation of Indian Chambers of Commerce and Industry (FICCI) to the United States (FICCI, United States, 1993), we stayed at hotels where the conferences were being held. This made it convenient for me to visit the conference halls before the event and check out the venue, examine the facilities, and generally get a sense of the place. This 'pre-visit' made a big difference in reassuring me about my performance. Here familiarity bred comfort and ease.

## FINALLY

It always helps to know beforehand details like the size of the conference hall, the number and location of entry and exit points, the seating arrangements, the placement of the stage, podium, lectern, and background screen, the availability of audiovisual facilities, and other arrangements, so that you can adjust your speaking style accordingly.

CHAPTER 20

# QUIETING THE MIND

*Listen to Classical and Meditative Music*

How should you prepare yourself on the day of the speech? Even an experienced speaker will get butterflies in the stomach before an important speaking event. It is therefore necessary to quiet the mind on the day of the speech. There are many ways of doing this, such as yoga, meditation, music therapy, stretching exercises, visualization, and deep breathing.

## YOGA

Yoga is an extremely popular, effective, and convenient method for achieving a state of relaxation and for reducing stress. Perform a set of yogic asanas and breathing exercises called pranayama in the morning of the day you are giving your speech and you will reap the benefits almost instantly.

Yoga has many techniques of breathing, all of which you can follow. The most well-known pranayamas are kabalbhati, anulom vilom, and brahmari.

My Delhi-based yoga practitioner and naturopath, Bipin Kumar Singh, has taught me anulom vilom, a breathing exercise that I do regularly and find particularly relaxing.

Here is how to do anulom vilom. Inhale deeply through the left nostril and exhale through the same nostril, keeping the right nostril closed with a finger or thumb. Repeat a few times. Now do the same with the right nostril. Repeat a few times.

Now inhale through the left nostril (keeping the right nostril closed) and exhale through the right nostril (keeping the left nostril closed). Repeat a few times. Now do the same with the right nostril. Inhale through the right nostril (keeping the left nostril closed) and exhale through the left nostril (keeping the right nostril closed). Repeat a few times.

## MEDITATION

The most universally accepted and regularly used technique for quieting the mind is meditation. There is nothing like meditation for improving your mood, focus, and concentration. Meditation teaches you to be calm and relaxed even in distracting or stressful conditions. The peace, serenity, and tranquility you experience after a session of daily meditation makes you more patient and understanding in your relations with others. Use the power of this powerful mental technique to quiet your mind. A round of meditation in the morning before the speaking event is highly recommended. Again, my yoga teacher, Bipin Kumar Singh, has successfully initiated me into the basic forms of meditation.

## CLASSICAL AND MEDITATIVE MUSIC

Listening to classical and meditative music in the morning can be soothing and calming.

Sound therapies have long been popular as a way of relaxing and unwinding. For centuries, indigenous cultures around the world have used music to enhance well-being and to improve health. Music is easily and readily available, so do use music to reduce stress, soothe your nerves, and sharpen your concentration whenever you have time.

What type of music should you choose? It all depends on your personal preference and taste. It could be Indian classical music, Western classical music, instrumental music, spa relaxing music, meditative music, or yoga relaxing music. I once had a sleeping problem and went to see a well-known doctor, who put me on to Mozart's classical music therapy. I was expecting a prescription for some drug; instead I got a prescription for music. It worked very well for me.

## OTHER TECHNIQUES FOR QUIETING THE MIND

If you have time, do some stretching exercises in the morning before you give your speech. Exercises can burn away tension and anxiety. Concentrate on a few exercises for lips, tongue, mouth, and jaw.

Give yourself enough time to dress well, with no hurry or stress. Once groomed and properly dressed, you will feel confident and relaxed.

Another technique I use is to visualize my earlier successful presentations and draw inspiration from the appreciation shown by the audience. Recall your previous successful presentations in as much detail as possible and enjoy the memory of the applause of your listeners.

If you wish, run through your speech one last time.

## DEEP BREATHING

As I begin my journey to the conference hall or speaking venue, I start the process of deep breathing, or stress-controlled breathing. This is often referred to as diaphragmatic breathing or abdominal breathing. If you inhale slowly and deeply and then breathe out slowly in a controlled way, you can relax your entire body. Do this repeatedly for as long as you can. The increased oxygen in your lungs eases your mind, relaxes your body, and boosts your energy. This type of breathing is used by stage actors, singers, athletes, speakers, and others to quiet the mind and to develop an overall feeling of wellness.

While I await my turn to speak, I start deep breathing again to quiet the mind and relax and to rid my system of any pent-up nervous energy. Take one or two deep breaths just before walking forward or standing up to give your presentation. Stress-controlled breathing helps you feel centred and inwardly calm.

## FINALLY

All these activities to quiet the mind should be done on the day of the speech: yoga, meditation, music therapy, stretching exercises, dressing well, visualization, and deep breathing. I have always benefitted enormously from them and I am sure you too will gain tremendously by adopting them. If you do all these activities on the morning of D-Day, you will succeed in putting yourself into the right frame of mind to make your speech persuasive and compelling. If you do not have time to do *all* of them, at least do some of them.

# Part Two

# PRESENTATION

CHAPTER 21

# SPEAKING STYLE

*A Piece of Paper cannot Stand between Me and Those I Want to Impress*

There are three different methods that you can use to deliver a speech:

- Reading the speech
- Memorizing the speech
- Speaking extempore (or planned improvisation)

## READING THE SPEECH

Have you ever been in an audience and heard speakers read out their speeches? They read, read, and read, rarely looking up and ignoring the audience. Try reading out a speech without engaging with your listeners and see how quickly the audience loses interest. They will soon start fidgeting and whispering amongst themselves.

Reading may be appropriate in some circumstances, like when you are making a formal announcement and at memorials when you need to be precise and careful in the words you use. But these are usually specific occasions.

Never read your speeches because it prevents you from being natural, conversational, and intimate with your audience. It stops you from making eye contact with your listeners because you do not look up, and hence you cannot gauge audience interest and engagement. It makes reaching out and connecting with your audience an uphill task. Pay heed to this wise counsel: *A piece of paper cannot stand between me and those I want to impress.*

1. *Your speech will become a monologue.* When you read your speech, it becomes a monologue. Remember, your audience can also read, so you might as well hand out copies of your speech; then everyone can sit in silence reading the speech together.

   There is a difference between the written word and the spoken word; something that reads well may not be as impressive when delivered orally. Opinion pieces, editorials, essays, briefs, legal argumentation, and the like may appear best in professional journals and newspapers, and may not necessarily be ideal material for speeches. Spoken speech is short, direct, and conversational.
2. *The audience will switch off.* There is nothing more boring than listening to someone reading a speech word for word. You can be sure the audience will switch off. Some will slouch in their seats; some will fidget; some will look out of the window; some will give side glances of boredom; some will doodle; some will play with their smart phones; and some will just go to sleep.
3. *You will be oblivious to the body language of the audience.* A self-absorbed speaker reading mechanically from a prepared text, in excruciating detail, has his head down and hence is oblivious to the body language of his audience, and will never be a good communicator. A good speaker will always be alert to the body language and reaction of his audience and will take steps to draw them in, especially if he observers that they are losing interest and are no longer engaged.

4. *Lincoln on the importance of animation and engagement.* Lincoln once said, 'I don't like to hear cut and dried sermons. No—when I hear a man preach, I like to see him act as if he were fighting bees.' What he meant was that he wanted to hear a speaker cut loose and get excited. No speaker will be able to do this if he is in the habit of reading speeches.

## MEMORIZING THE SPEECH

Do not try to memorize an entire speech. All your energy will be directed inwards instead of outwards to your audience. Your talk will sound mechanical and will lack the vital ingredients of enthusiasm and spontaneity.

Here we can learn from Churchill who was not a natural-born speaker. When he started his career, he had a slight stammer which he overcame through will power and practice to become one of the most brilliant orators of the twentieth century. When a young man, Churchill wrote out and memorized his speeches. One day when giving his first speech at the age of thirty in the House of Commons, he tried to speak entirely from memory, but soon forgot his lines. His mind went blank and his face turned scarlet. He had to sit down in embarrassment and humiliation.

After this disastrous experience, Churchill vowed never to give a memorized speech again. Instead, he would spend hours preparing and practising a single speech, working and reworking it until he finally thought it perfect. His friend Lord Birkenhead joked, 'Winston has spent the best years of his life writing impromptu speeches.' At the height of World War II, Churchill's morale-boosting speeches went a long way in sustaining the British people.

## SPEAKING EXTEMPORE (OR PLANNED IMPROVISATION)

This method requires delivering what appears to be an extempore speech, but it is backed by hours of solid practice, hence it is often referred to as planned improvisation.

1. *Speaking with prompt cards.* Speaking extempore (or planned improvisation) is backed by hours of thorough preparation and extensive rehearsal. The idea is to sound natural and at ease, but without reading from a prepared script. I like to give my speeches extempore, but supported by prompt cards on which I note the main points related to the theme of my talk for reference. Do not write the entire speech word for word in the prompt cards. Instead, note down ideas. As you finish discussing one idea, glance at your prompt cards merely as an aid to your memory (if you need it) and move to the next idea. Articulate your ideas extempore. Do not read and do not attempt to memorize the exact words that you are going to use.
2. *Learn to express your key points in more than one way.* Practise articulating your main proposals using words that come naturally to you, without attempting to memorize the speech word for word. After repeated rehearsals, you will find yourself speaking fluently and coherently, describing your proposals in different words and in different ways. In this manner, you will cement the expression of those proposals in your mind, and also learn the skill of improvising and speaking spontaneously. Learn to communicate your message from many different perspectives. Learn to have more than one way of expressing your key points. Rehearse at least a dozen times so that you can lucidly present the propositions in a natural and easy manner without in particular trying to memorize the exact words. Memorize the ideas, but let the words flow in any sequence.

Of course, this does not mean that you should not attempt to use certain pre-identified words for effect. Certain words have a cadence and rhythm, and hence an appeal. Certainly, you may memorize such single words, or a series of words, and use them to make your presentation more successful. For example, use picture words or rhetorical devices like anaphora or alliteration (these techniques are discussed elsewhere in this book).

3. *It is easier to engage with the audience.* When you are not tied to a written text, but are speaking extempore from prompt cards, you are personalizing your speech. The audience is on the edge of engagement. You scan the audience and note audience interest or lack thereof. You detect signs of agreement or you see impatient fidgeting with sideways glances of disinterest. Alerted to this alarming situation, you can change gears and become reactive to the audience, perhaps by changing pace, or pausing, or moving on to another, more interesting proposition, or improvising. It is easier to engage your listeners when you have both eyes scanning and looking at the audience. All this is not possible when you are reading a speech.
4. *Rehearse.* Practice is the key to giving excellent extempore speeches. Unless you have a supreme gift, it is very unlikely that you will be able to achieve excellence in speaking without putting in hours and hours of hard drill. If you think that you can just stand on your feet and dazzle an audience, particularly in a formal arena, without adequate preparation, you will soon be disabused of this idea. Speakers have been known to carry their script everywhere, rehearsing from it in cars, in airplanes, in hotel rooms, as often as they can (sometimes even fifty times), to get the flow of the speech just right. Sometimes for important presentations, or negotiations, speakers

start thinking about the event and the audience perhaps two or three months before.

Of course, exactly when you start working on your speech before D-Day will depend on the significance you attach to the event. An annual partners' meeting or an annual dealers' meeting may get you moving months in advance, whereas preparing a few opening remarks for a visiting dignitary may take just a few days.

5. *Speaking without prompt cards.* This is a slight variant of the method of giving a speech with prompt cards. The process is the same. You practise your speech with prompt cards, except that on D-Day you do not carry them with you.

Speaking extempore without prompt cards is fine if you can pull it off successfully. When you have gained sufficient experience, try giving your speech with no prompt cards whatsoever. If you have spent enough time practising the enunciation, timing, gesturing, and so on, you will find that giving speeches without prompt cards is not a difficult task. It may appear hard the first time, but if you prepare well by using the various techniques described in this book, you will succeed easily with no prompt cards. It is all in the mind. It is a matter of confidence.

Once you have a reasonable number of successful speeches under your belt, ask yourself how often you actually referred to the prompt cards. You will find that you hardly consulted them at all. So why not just leave the prompt cards at home or in the office on D-Day? Regard your prompt cards as a safety net and nothing more. When you realize that you glance at them only occasionally, and that too only out of habit, rather than actually reading from them, you will stop carrying them around.

When you get back from a speaking event, recall the speech that you have just given without the prompt cards, without the actual script, to ascertain whether you had left out any parts. You will be surprised to discover that you hardly left out anything important. But the key to be able to do this is hours and hours of unrelenting practice and rehearsal.

## FINALLY

I end this chapter with two appropriate quotes. Mark Twain, the well-known American writer, said: 'It usually takes me more than three weeks to prepare a good impromptu speech.' Pat O'Malley, an American actor, put it humorously: 'I know better than to make speeches. I am reminded of the famous doctor who once said: "Speeches are like babies—easy to conceive, hard to deliver!"'

CHAPTER 22

# TAKING POSSESSION OF YOUR TERRITORY

*A Long Pause Establishes your Presence and Status*

Think about marking your presence on the stage. When your name is announced, get up from your chair only after the announcement has been completed, and not when it is still taking place. Do not be in a rush to get to the podium. Walk to the podium with your normal pace, neither fast nor slow. Do not acknowledge the applause that may greet your name.

## TAKE YOUR TIME

Once at the podium, take your time to settle in: remain silent, stand straight and solid, breathe calmly, adjust the microphone, place your prompt cards on the podium and gaze down at them whether you need to or not. You may be tempted to start speaking there and then, but resist this. Prolong these few seconds further with the process of settling in. There is no hurry. Fill the stage with your presence. In other words, *take possession of your territory.* Sweep the auditorium with your confident gaze. Do not start speaking in a rush. Take your time, settle in, let the audience settle in, and then start speaking.

## HOLD BACK A LITTLE

Taking possession of your territory requires some practice. It requires a conscious effort to hold back a little bit. It is a natural tendency for speakers to reach the podium and start speaking instantly. The nervous speaker wants to start right away. The skilled speaker waits. It is natural to be a little ill at ease with silence, but try to overcome this apprehension. A little deliberation; a little pause; a little fixing of the microphone to get it in a proper position—it all adds up to give an impression of being in control. So resist the initial urge to start your speech at once. A lot depends on those first few minutes when you fill the stage with your presence.

## NEVER RUSH THE CHAIRMAN

Never rush the chairman or show impatience, even if the chairman's introduction is a bit long-winded. This sometimes happens when the speaker thinks his status is higher than that of the chairman. This happened to me once when I was introducing a speaker who was getting impatient and trying to hurry me on in my introductory remarks. Such behaviour is unbecoming of a speaker, who at all times must remain composed and patient. The speaker should get up only when the introduction has been completed. Then the speaker must take possession of his territory, slowly and deliberately.

## FINALLY

*A long pause establishes your presence and status.* It gives the audience time to look you over. It is a powerful way to begin. You appear firmly in control.

# CHAPTER 23

## STANCE

Do not Slouch

Express your presence through your posture. *Do not slouch.* Stand erect and stay still. Adopt a balanced stance. Make sure the weight is evenly distributed between both feet. This projects authority and self-assurance. Never lean on a hip, either left or right. Never slump. Never grasp the podium as though for support or in desperation. Never place an elbow heavily on the podium. Avoid all awkward mannerisms and distracting postures, so that the audience can concentrate on what you are saying instead of watching your strange antics.

### INCORRECT STANCE

During the course of listening to many speeches, I have come across many different types of stances. I have seen speakers push one side of their body forward, so that their stance is askew and out of alignment. Some lean heavily on the podium as if seeking support. Some stand with their weight on one leg and the other knee bent, adopting a casual demeanour which detracts from their authority. Some lean slightly backwards, which makes them look aloof. Some stand with their arms pressed close to the body, which makes them look insecure and anxious to please, and which also undercuts their authority. Some shuffle around the podium restlessly. Some speak away from the podium, walking back and forth, crisscrossing the stage, which is distracting to the audience.

## CORRECT STANCE

The correct posture is to stand with feet apart, evenly balanced, with equal weight on each foot, and with the weight on the heels and balls of both feet. The weight should be evenly distributed from side to side and from front to back. Stand erect; do not slouch. The balanced stance actually decreases tension because it distributes the weight evenly on both sides of the body. Two legs are better than one at supporting body weight. Let your hands fall lightly and naturally on either side of the body, or rest them lightly on the podium. Do not fold your hands behind the back, like a policeman, or in front in a fig-leaf position. The balanced stance is your home base; it is where you start and where you return. It is a solid position from which solid statements can be made.

Standing is preferable to sitting, unless decorum requires that the speaker be seated. Standing is more authoritative than sitting. It enables better eye contact and more efficient breathing. If you choose to sit, make sure to follow all the principles that apply when you are standing: maintain a balanced stance and stay settled, with feet on the ground. The most common mistake that people make when in a sitting position is to lean back, which makes them appear uninvolved and disinterested. Do not lean back; lean slightly forward, with your energy flowing towards the audience.

Once when I arrived to give a speech, I found that there was no stage and no podium and that there was about twelve feet of open space between me and the front row of the audience. I adopted my usual balanced stance in the middle and made this my home base. I treated this position as my imaginary podium. Luckily, I had decided to speak without prompt cards, so that I had both my hands free for hand gestures.

## PHYSICAL ASPECTS OF THE SPEAKING SITUATION

Sometimes you may not have enough information about all the physical aspects of the speaking situation, like the size of the stage, the position of the audience, and the location of the podium. In such circumstances, you have to make impromptu decisions about the most appropriate position and stance, and treat the incident as a learning experience for the next time such a situation arises.

The accomplished speaker is comfortable speaking regardless of the physical aspects of the speaking situation. Generally, the invitation to speak should provide all the necessary details, but in case there is uncertainty, ask for more information. Will there be a stage with chairman and co-speakers? Will there be a podium? Will there be an overhead projector? Will there be any barriers between the speaker and the audience?

## PERSONAL EXAMPLE

Only once have I been really caught unawares. This was a presentation to the Central Board of Direct Taxes (CBDT, New Delhi, 1995). There was no podium or stage, but only a U-shaped arrangement of chairs. I was for a few minutes puzzled as to how to take my stance. Should I speak from where I was seated or should I move to the front of the U-shape? Such makeshift arrangements are only likely to arise in the case of presentations before small audiences. Since I was speaking for the first time to the CBDT, I should have checked in advance on the seating and speaking arrangements, which I had failed to do.

## CONCLUSION

Finally, in your training sessions, use a balanced stance as you stand in a familiar room and rehearse your speech. A balanced stance with equal weight on both feet conveys authority and poise and enables correct breathing. It is the preferred position taken by skilled and experienced speakers. It allows you the security of owning your own space. It conveys to the audience that you know what you are talking about. It allows you to be more relaxed and aware of the audience.

CHAPTER 24

# CHOREOGRAPHY

From your Base, Make Occasional Minor or Major Sorties

Choreography is a way of using your speaking space—the physical area around the podium, or, if there is no podium, around your imaginary podium—to your maximum advantage. The space available for you to use may be to the left or to the right of the podium, or even a few steps back. Space will also be available at the front, close to the audience. You can also create space (or at least the illusion of space) by moving from a standing posture behind the podium to a sitting posture (on a chair or stool) in the centre of the stage. *From your base, make occasional minor or major sorties.*

## MINOR SORTIES: MOVING AROUND AND ABOUT THE PODIUM

Most speakers tend to stick behind the podium for the entire speech. However, your stance as the speaker does not mean that you have to remain rooted to the podium for the entire duration of your time on the stage. Experienced and skilled speakers will depart from the podium on a few occasions and move to a different space on the stage, thereby breaking the monotony and stasis of staying put in one place and adding dynamism and energy by moving around. It is a good idea to make minor sorties away from the podium; these may be to the right or to the left of the podium, but should be done sparingly and with a definite purpose in mind like adding emphasis to a point, reading a quotation, posing a rhetorical question, synchronizing your movement with a deliberate pause, or signalling a transition from one idea to another.

When you make your sorties away from the podium, do not partially step aside from the podium, so that you are partly visible and partly hidden, and are half-blocked from view. To the audience, this may imply some form of concealment on your part. Wherever you go—to the left of the podium or to the right—get there with deliberateness and then plant your feet firmly on the floor. Do not shuffle or fidget or move around needlessly. The shift in position should be timed. The shifting of position should not be more than twice or thrice in a forty-five-minute speaking session.

## MAJOR SORTIES: WALKING TO THE FRONT OF THE STAGE, AS CLOSE AS POSSIBLE TO THE AUDIENCE

At times, move away from the podium to the front of the stage, but with purpose and a clear intention of making an important point or reference. When abandoning the podium, get completely clear of it and walk to the front, as close as possible to the audience as the stage permits, exposing yourself completely—breast, stomach, and loins. This indicates candour, confidence, and ease on your part. Such forays away from the podium and to the front should be infrequent and must be made with a clear focus and concrete intent. Perhaps you need to get an important message across to your audience that warrants your moving upstage to the very edge of the stage, in order to get as close to the audience as possible.

Major departures from the podium must be accompanied by the sharing of some very important message. This movement creates variety, energy, dynamism, and flow, and hence will be noticed, so you had better have something significant to say. This is especially important when you are taking questions. Standing without a physical barrier in front of you makes you seem more open to the audience and they will be encouraged to listen to you, engage with you, and ask questions.

Choreography may also be required if a section of the audience does not seem to be listening as carefully as the rest of the assembled crowd. Moving into their space for just a few moments will often encourage them to give up their private conversation and will bring their attention back to you.

However, do not be too rigid in following a preset pattern of movement. Allow yourself impulsive, impromptu departures from the podium if the mood is such that it feels the right thing to do. But do not walk and talk at the same time. Do not talk while you are in movement from the podium to the front and when you return to the podium. Return to the podium and then resume your discourse. Be careful never to turn your shoulders or your back to the audience.

## FINALLY

How does choreography work in practice? You want to first study your speech to find the high points. What are the two or three moments in the speech that are the most important? It is when you are discussing these points that you want to be in the personal space of a selected section of the audience—perhaps to the left or to the right of the stage or in front. Plan your choreography in advance. Plot your movements across the stage. Rehearse these movements at home. Highlight these in your prompt cards.

I hope that you have understood the choreography that is involved in delivering a speech. Use the space around the podium to your advantage. You want to move towards select members of the audience before making a major point, an emphatic declaration, or an important announcement. By getting nearer, you are alerting the audience that something big is coming up. Often it can lead to tremendous audience awareness and anticipation. Try it and see the results for yourself.

# CHAPTER 25

## SMILE

*A Smile can Radiate Through the Room*

Smiling coupled with eye contact is a great way to make a first good impression. Give a big, broad, and heartfelt smile to establish a quick rapport with the audience. Look at people directly and smile. *A smile can radiate through the room.* Even unhappy or grouchy people will smile right back. Smiles are contagious.

### THE PODIUM IS NOT THE PLACE FOR A POKER FACE

A speaker with a blank, expressionless face makes the task of connecting with the audience that much harder. A deadpan expression is a recipe for disaster. If you are an impassive speaker, learn to relax. Lift the muscles near the mouth and cheeks. If your brows are knitted, relax them. Try not to scowl or frown.

There is a natural tendency at moments of stress not to smile. You must work hard at smiling even though you may be under strain because a smile can light up a room and make the audience eager to hear what you have to say. In case you tend to forget to smile, mark places in your prompt cards reminding yourself to smile through your presentation. A good way to know whether you tend to smile or not is to ask a confidant in the audience to give you feedback or, better still, to video record yourself.

Anyone who was taught that a display of emotions in public is unseemly and was urged to present an impassive countenance to the world will not make much headway with audiences. Sometimes people do not allow their faces to express their natural feelings for social or professional reasons. However, the podium is not the place for a poker face. Allow your natural self to emerge and greet people with a warm smile, a welcoming expression, and a positive attitude. This openness will spread to others and they too will reciprocate with a smile. Try delivering speeches expressing various emotions like elation, sorrow, joy, anger, curiosity, anticipation.

## LEARN THE ART OF SMILING

In reality, we all have different personalities which we express in different ways as we go through our daily life. Some people tend to laugh or smile more; some are quick to anger; and some are just miserable and edgy. If you want to be a successful speaker, no matter what your personality, you must learn the art of smiling, as this will endear you straight away to your audience and make your task of reaching out and communicating effectively much easier. Of course, there are occasions when it would not be appropriate to smile, for example, at a funeral oration or eulogy.

Learn to smile pleasantly straight away when you arrive for the speaking event. A person with a smile is always welcome. Remember, if you smile, others will smile back. The smile indicates confidence and self-esteem, warmth and friendliness. It shows that you are looking forward to the event and are ready to mix with the audience.

Mother Teresa, the nun and missionary leader, reminds us: 'Let us always meet each other with a smile, for the smile is the beginning of love.'

Mark Twain, the well-known American writer, echoes this: 'Never regret anything that made you smile.'

## FINALLY

A poem sometimes attributed to the American self-improvement writer Dale Carnegie captures the essence of a smile wonderfully well: 'It costs nothing, but creates much. It enriches those who receive, without impoverishing those who give. It happens in a flash and the memory of it sometimes lasts forever. None are so rich they can get along without it and none so poor but are richer for its benefits.'

CHAPTER 26

# EYE CONTACT

*Individualize Members of the Audience Through Eye Contact*

As you speak, establish eye contact with members of the audience. Move your head slowly, shifting your gaze from one side of the room to the centre and then to the other side, spending a few moments focusing on the main body of people in each section of the room. As you speak, select four or five individuals for attention and speak directly to them, establishing eye contact. However, do not ignore any section of the audience. Eye contact is not about shifting your head to follow the movement of the ball in a tennis match and nor does it mean scanning the audience quickly. Rather, it involves actually speaking to, or addressing your remarks at, a particular individual or individuals in the audience for a few seconds and then transferring your attention to other people seated elsewhere in the room.

## INADEQUATE EYE CONTACT

I have seen speakers look over the heads of people in the audience. I have seen speakers look only at their notes and never at their audience. I have seen speakers ignore sections of the audience. Such speakers will never be as productive or as impressive as they could be had they established proper eye contact. They reduce their own effectiveness as communicators by not establishing eye contact with their listeners.

In many conference halls, the podium is set on either the left or the right side of the room, and seldom in the centre. The natural tendency for the speaker, therefore, is to speak to the section of the audience facing him and to ignore the other side. Nothing is more disconcerting to an audience than to be ignored and to be found seated in the wrong side of the hall. This results in one part of the audience being fully absorbed in the speech and the other part becoming restless, fidgeting and doodling. Make a conscious effort to speak to sections of the audience on both sides of the hall, ignoring neither side, otherwise the ignored side will go to sleep. If you do not pay attention to your audience, they will not pay attention to you.

## DIVIDE THE CROWD INTO FOUR ZONES OR QUARTERS AND INDIVIDUALIZE MEMBERS OF THE AUDIENCE

Eye contact means looking into the eyes of selected audience members, and not glancing at them vaguely or in passing. It means identifying and recognizing the expression on their faces. It means recognizing the colour of their clothes. It means establishing a personal, intimate relation with them. *Individualize members of the audience.* Practise looking at each person for at least two to three seconds. If this is too difficult at first, practise on objects at home. Learn to gauge the actual duration of an eye rest lasting two to three seconds. After your speech, try to remember how individuals looked. Who frowned? Who smiled? Who nodded? If you can recall the facial expressions of specific people, you are making good eye contact.

Never conceive of an audience as a sea of anonymous faces. Obviously, you cannot look at all the members of an audience. The speaker cannot surf the audience, but must single people out for attention. He should divide the crowd into four zones and select an interesting person in each zone and then speak to that person at a personal level, one to one. There must be personal bonding through the eyes with selected individuals in the hall. However, when you look at one individual in a particular section of the hall, it will convey your recognition of that person from your vantage point, or official position, as a speaker to all the other people sitting in the vicinity of that individual. As the speaker fastens his attention on one person, others nearby get the impression that the speaker is also concentrating on them. In this manner, the speaker should cover all the zones in the hall. The speaker should strive to achieve a personal engagement, and it is in this manner that the speaker exercises control over the audience. In this way, the speaker identifies with the audience and the audience identifies with the speaker and his message.

## BILL CLINTON AND THE IMPORTANCE OF EYE CONTACT

Many have said of Bill Clinton, a former president of the United States, that he was the greatest political communicator they ever saw. Paying attention with his eyes was his secret weapon. Psychologists call eye contact the strongest form of non-verbal communication. Clinton's intense eye contact was a powerful display of his attention to others and of his inherent ability to connect. This sympathetic trait of identifying with others through direct and respectful eye contact can make you more effective in every aspect of your life.

## EYES EXPRESS EMOTIONS

Looking at someone directly demonstrates that you are interested in them. Consider some common phrases about people in love: 'she has eyes only for him'; 'they could not take their eyes off each other'. If you see two people talking together, you can gauge how intimate they are by observing the extent of their eye contact. With eye contact, we indicate our concern or indifference, like or dislike, boredom or interest, and even hatred and animosity, as in 'if looks could kill' and 'she looked daggers at him'. We express our emotions through our eyes.

## EYE CONTACT DENOTES AUTHORITY

Eye contact also denotes authority. Confident people engage in more frequent eye contact than those who are less confident. Skilful speakers by selecting different individuals around the hall can cover the entire audience. If you establish eye contact with just ten people in an audience of a hundred, it is said that you have won over the audience. Remember this 1:10 ratio. So, with an audience of fifty, try making eye contact with only five people to establish control over the entire gathering of fifty individuals.

## PRACTISE EYE CONTACT

Practise eye contact in daily conversation, so that you get into the habit of establishing eye contact with all those you encounter. You will have plenty of opportunities to establish eye contact with people you meet daily. A good way to start is by making eye contact with strangers, like waiters, sales clerks, cashiers, and other paid service staff, so long as you do it respectfully and in a friendly way. Do not be aggressive, rude, or intrusive. The idea is not to stare down people so that they feel uncomfortable, threatened, or bullied. Start slowly. Make eye contact initially for a few seconds only. Then increase the amount of time you make eye contact. Little by little, it will become less of an issue, less of a barrier. Soon it will become second nature to you. It will come automatically. But it requires practice.

## EYE CONTACT IN WILDLIFE PHOTOGRAPHY

Even in wildlife photography, eye contact is critical. Aim for the eyes is the constant refrain of the wildlife photographer. By ensuring that the eyes are the main focal point in your photograph, you can make the shot extremely powerful. Eye contact also helps reveal the personality of the animal being photographed and lets the viewer connect with the animal. Being able to look straight into the eyes of a tiger or lion helps build a sense of intimacy and offers a glimpse into the personality or soul of the animal. The eyes show whether the animal is agitated and angry, unconcerned and bored, fearful and nervous, shy and timid, or hungry and tired. The eyes can also show triumph and dominance. Make no mistake, the eyes of an animal communicate. They are no different than human eyes.

## CONCLUSION

The principles of making eye contact are the same whether you are talking to five people, five hundred, or five thousand. You will find that when you establish eye contact, you will be taken more seriously and will be in a better position to get your message across.

Accomplished speakers through eye bonding achieve this personal engagement with and control over the audience. This is how the small presence of one speaker addressing a large audience grows in magnitude until the speaker dominates, or connects with, the audience. Try it for yourself and see the impressive results.

Using your eyes is a great communication tool. Work hard at honing your eye-contact skills and it will pay rich dividends in enabling contact with your audience and in reaching them with your message. Good eye contact can command attention, focus, and respect. Eye contact conveys authority and expertise, signals that you are comfortable and relaxed with the speaking situation, and reveals poise and confidence. It is an important element, and an indispensable step, in becoming a powerful and compelling speaker.

## FINALLY

To disregard the power of eye contact is not an option. This is one technique that you ignore at the risk of failure of becoming an effective communicator. If you shut your eyes to this tool of communication, you may forfeit the ability to make brilliant speeches. It has been said that 'eye contact beats any conversation'. How true!

CHAPTER 27

# VOICE

*Master the Art of Modulating and Animating your Voice*

This chapter deals with articulation, pace, modulation, inflection, and voice flexibility. Variety in voice can be achieved by pace, volume, tone, phrase, and pause. Phrase and pause are discussed in detail in other chapters.

## ARTICULATION

Articulation, the act of shaping sounds into words and enunciating words clearly, imparts the qualities of energy and authority to the voice. For good articulation, speak clearly and energetically with an open mouth. Get involved with the sound of the words. Be in control of the process of producing and uttering words. I have heard speakers who mumble and speak indistinctly, with listlessness and lack of energy. Others clench their teeth so hard that the sound that emerges is muffled. A good way of achieving proper articulation is to utter your words as if you were speaking to people who can only lip read. This exercise may seem strange at first, but is a proven method of improving articulation.

## VERBAL DELIVERY

Verbal delivery consists of the following elements:

- Speed (pace) at which you speak

- Volume—loud or soft
- Tone—high or low inflection
- Use of phrase
- Use of pause

## VOICE MODULATION

**Master the art of modulating and animating your voice.** Your voice should vary in volume, tone, pitch, pace, and emphasis. Cultivate the art of animating your voice to attract and hold the audience's attention. Learn how to use the downward inflection and the pause to communicate more effectively.

## PACE

Many people have a natural tendency to speak fast, swallowing words and eliding sounds. This is a no-no in public speaking. Force yourself to slow down and regulate the pace of your speech during practice. Variation in pace adds to the speaker's authority and enhances audience listenability. When you practise, a good rule is to speak so slowly that it feels unnatural. Identify passages where slowness and deliberateness are required, and passages that call for speed and velocity. Speech must be slowed down or hurried forward, or held back in brief or long pauses, or accelerated or decelerated as often as the text demands.

Vocal flexibility and versatility are also needed to address the acoustics in the conference room. The larger the room, the slower you must speak.

The speaker should travel according to the load being carried and the steepness of the ground. A relentless march forward at the same pace is monotonous and boring, not to say exhausting. The audience expects a halt by the wayside from time to time. Among the wide range of technical requirements for effective public speaking, varied pace is difficult to achieve but is necessary for the art of voice modulation. It is essential for the public speaker to master varied pace.

Slow down the pace in the following instances:

- when explaining something complicated
- when talking about a grave matter
- when giving data and statistics
- when clarifying a point or statement

Speed up the pace in the following instances:

- when narrating the end or climax of a story
- when giving examples or illustrations
- when delivering the less important parts of your speech

## DOWNWARD INFLECTION

You can add authority and assurance to your voice with downward inflection. Downward inflection makes your words sound definite, confident, and persuasive. Inflection is the way you vary or modulate the pitch and tone of your voice, especially at the end of a word, phrase or sentence, according to the meaning and emphasis you wish to impart. As a general rule, when the sense is clear and complete, there is a downward inflection. This does not mean changing the pitch of the voice suddenly and jerkily, but means just a general trend. Start with a higher pitch and then slowly lower it, so the sound moves in a downward curve. Try this technique first in casual one-to-one conversation. Mark the places in a chosen text where you feel downward inflection is required and then voice record yourself reading it.

## UPWARD INFLECTION

In contrast, when the sense is unclear and incomplete, there is an upward inflection. Upward inflection, the tilt to a higher pitch at the end of a word or at the end of a sentence, carries the sense and sound of a question, as if the speaker is unsure. Upward inflection undercuts your authority and indicates uncertainty, insecurity, hesitation, and doubt. Use an upward inflection when asking a question: 'Was this ambition?' Or when making an appeal: 'Good friends, sweet friends, let me not stir you up to such a sudden flood of mutiny.' (Mark Antony, in *Julius Caesar*, Act 3, Scene 2).

## PRACTICE

Record yourself speaking and then play back the recording so you can analyse your performance. It is important to hear the sound of your voice if you want to improve it. Practising this way will really help you identify your strengths and weaknesses as a public speaker. Look for variation in the voice, look for pace, look for change in tone, look for downward inflection, look for proper phrasing, look for pause. Above all, look for enthusiasm and vitality. Does your voice sound strong and interesting, lively and engaging? The more you hear yourself, the more ideas you will have for improving your style and delivery. Read poetry to free your voice. Reading Shakespeare's plays is excellent training for developing a flexible and expressive voice.

## VOICE FLEXIBILITY

Eat sparingly before your speech. When you are hungry, your body releases adrenaline which will key you up even more. Overeating before a speech will make you sluggish. Avoid dairy products like ice cream, cheese, and even tea or coffee with milk as they coat your mouth and throat and can give you an unpleasant voice, causing your voice to crack.

Be cautious about what you drink before a speech. To ensure the best possible voice, drink only room-temperature or warm water prior to and during your speech. Avoid cold water, which causes your vocal cords to contract, making your voice less flexible. Soft drinks with sugar are also not good for your voice. Warm water or plain tea is best.

Do not drink alcohol. Speeches are often preceded by drinks or cocktails, or it could be a dinner speech. Having a cold drink might seem like a good idea, even if you have remembered to avoid alcohol. However, even a cold drink can sometimes play havoc with your vocal cords. Of course, all this is easier said than done. I myself have broken this rule unintentionally a few times and paid the price.

## QUICK FIX

For your next speech, try a quick fix by introducing variety into your voice. Here is how you can do this:

- Read a passage fast. Vary your speed at least once.
- Insert a dramatic pause after the most important point in your speech.
- Before the pause, use downward inflection of the voice.
- Just before the conclusion, use downward inflection of the voice.
- Put a rhetorical question into your speech. Your voice will rise naturally.

## CONCLUSION

If the pace, volume, pitch, inflection, and rhythm of your voice never fluctuate, you will be speaking with no voice modulation, and hence in a monotone, and you will lose your audience as a result. A monotone suggests to your listeners that you are not prepared to expend the energy necessary to connect with them. It indicates that you do not really care much whether or how your listeners respond.

Once you adopt a regular routine of voice exercises and other techniques as described above, the result will be evident even in your everyday speech. Developing a powerful voice which conveys authority and energy, and is sensitive to the needs of audience awareness, will help you in communicating successfully with your audience.

Use an expressive voice which rises and falls in both volume and pitch, changes pace, moves between upward and downward inflection, pauses and quickens, and exhibits a range of emotions—from certainty to doubt, astonishment to acceptance, delight to disgust.

## FINALLY

The main part of your speech should display as many variations in pace, volume, and tone as the text demands. Employ voice modulation, a vital speaking technique that will enhance your presence and dominance in every speaking situation. Just as an artist or photographer uses shadows to accentuate light (say, bright sunshine juxtaposed against a dimly lit interior), likewise a good speaker varies his voice, tone, pitch, and pace to capture the attention of the audience.

If you can express enthusiasm and energy through your voice by varying it as the text demands, you will be able to hold the interest of your audience. Publilius Syrus, who flourished in the 1st century BC in Ancient Rome, said: 'Speech is the mirror of the soul; as a man speaks, so he is.'

CHAPTER 28

# PHRASE

Semi-Pauses are Necessary for Imparting Meaning and Rhythm

Phrasing is a group of words belonging closely together that are kept together in speaking and are not divided unnaturally by breath pauses in the middle. A sentence is made up of several short phrases of varying importance. The speaker should learn to think in terms of phrases when delivering a speech. Phrasing and emphasis are closely linked. A phrase is built around a particular word, and each emphasized word is the focus of interest in its own phrase.

## HOW TO PHRASE

If a long sentence is to be clearly understood, it should be divided into suitable phrases. This is done by making a slight break in the flow of breath to indicate the beginning of each new phrase. There should be no hold-up of the breath. These breaks are not to be considered as occasions for actual deep breathing, but they do afford, if required, an opportunity to replenish the lungs. The phrases are to be spoken without disturbing or disrupting the real continuity of the sentence.

Phrasing is the breaking up of a sentence through the use of semi-pauses as you speak. *These semi-pauses are necessary for imparting meaning and rhythm*, otherwise you will talk too fast, eliding your words, which is a common fault in public speaking. By introducing semi-pauses in a sentence, you bring in meaning and pacing, emphasis and cadence. The phrase pauses may not necessarily be of equal length. Some may be the merest suggestion of a pause; you may call this a half-phrase pause. Phrasing allows the speaker to be clearly understood by the audience, and hence is worth mastering.

## PRACTISE PHRASING

Here are two examples of phrasing, the grouping of similar words for effect. Practise saying the sentences out aloud, semi-pausing at the places separated by the four dots or ellipses, before continuing:

- 'I was delighted . . . . to accept your invitation . . . . to speak to you tonight . . . . and to give my views on the benefits . . . . which the Parkland Scheme will bring . . . . to the people of this district . . . . benefits I would say that have been long deserved . . . . and waited for.'
- 'Now . . . . his eldest son . . . . was in the field . . . . and as he came and drew nigh to the house . . . . he heard music and dancing . . . . and he called one of the servants . . . . and asked what these things meant.'

The best way of understanding and mastering the concept of phrasing is to read a script into a voice recorder and then listening carefully to the recording. Pick an interesting article from a newspaper and read it with proper phrasing as if you were making a speech. Then listen back to the recording so you can identify the places where you have used phrasing most effectively.

## CONCLUSION

Phrasing—the division made by the speaker of words into groups or units—is an important ingredient of style. Phrasing makes for a clearer understanding of the meaning of words, and indeed of the sentence. The speaker should know how to make intelligent use of phrasing in order to be clearly understood, otherwise he will end up confusing his audience.

The public speaker should cultivate phrasing until it becomes a habit, otherwise he may get entangled in delivering a lengthy and complicated sentence which seems to lead nowhere. Sentences built by phrasing are easy to understand, they are less taxing on the speaker as well as the audience, and they convey a sense of style. Your ability to speak the words of a phrase with lightness and briskness will boost your reputation as a speaker. You will be easily and clearly understood. Your speech will have a rhythm and cadence indicating confidence and assurance. Try to master the art of phrasing and see the improvement in your performance.

CHAPTER 29

# PAUSE

*The Skilful Use of the Pause is Essential to the Speaker's Craft*

In power speaking, the pause plays a critical role. This powerful attention-getter is one of the most effective devices at a speaker's command. To learn the art of the pause for effect is to understand how to convey authority and confidence. To pause either before or after an important statement is to enhance audience awareness significantly.

The skilful and experienced speaker knows how to use the pause for maximum effect, how and when to time it, and how long to hold it. He wields the pause as an essential tool to convey meaning and emphasis, and to build and then release audience interest. The sudden cessation of any sound produces an extraordinary effect. The power of the pause can be electrifying. The audience is left wondering what's next. Suspense holds people in their seats. Learn to relish the silence. Be in no rush. Take your time.

## PLAN FOR YOUR PAUSES

At a recent speech, I paused after asking a rhetorical question and I could feel the audience waiting in anticipation for the next words. People looked at me expectantly, as if waiting for an important statement.

Make sure to mark the places in your speaking notes where you need to pause and incorporate them in your rehearsal. Unless you are very skilled, and you have an instinct or natural sense about knowing when to pause at the right moment, it is best to plan for the pauses. I plan for my pauses. I use the pause at least once or twice in a forty-five-minute speech. Do not use it too often in the same speech.

## A PAUSE CAN BE EXTREMELY ELOQUENT

A pause is different from a break. A break is a natural progression from one structured part of the speech to another. A pause is aimed at emphasizing a particular point, either before or after the point.

Try to build this technique into your speaking style. A pause at the right place and at the right moment makes everyone attentive, alert, and eager to hear what will come next. Stop speaking suddenly, stand silently, look around, and hold the pause until you are ready to proceed. Make it dramatic. You have set the stage for what will follow next. The spotlight is on what you will now say. The statement to follow must be worthy of the pause. Try and follow the pause by speaking in a different tone of voice, adopting perhaps a downward inflection or even engaging in choreography. You can also pause after making the point, giving time for the meaning to sink in.

Powerful speakers use the pause strategically and wisely to achieve several goals—to emphasize, to create an effect, and to set a mood. Pauses can be long or short, as the mood directs. A dramatic pause can last anywhere from three to seven seconds. *A pause can be extremely eloquent.*

## PERSONAL EXAMPLE

In a speech on 'Frauds in India' at a talk organized for a select group of managers and partners at Chennai (EY, India, 2020), I narrated the story of Bernie Madoff, the American investment advisor and financier who ran the largest Ponzi scheme in history and the largest financial fraud in U.S. history. In his trial, Madoff had admitted to the fraud and was sentenced to 150 years in a federal prison. I had marked in my prompt cards the place where I wanted to pause. At the appropriate part of my speech, I asked the question: 'How long was Madoff sentenced to?' I paused. After the pause, I answered, 'One hundred and fifty years.'

By pausing and then holding the pause for some seconds before the mention of the 150 years, I created audience awareness and anticipation. I was comfortable with the pause. I relished the silence. I was in no hurry. If there were people in the audience whose minds were wandering, I am sure that with the pause I brought them back to focus on the talk.

The pause indicates the speaker's control of the speaking situation and displays his authority and dominance in terms of setting the pace and direction of the talk. *The skilful use of the pause is essential to the speaker's craft.*

## MORE EXAMPLES OF THE PAUSE

- Wait till I tell you the good news . . . (pause) . . . then tell them the good news.'
- If there is anyone of you that has not sinned . . . (pause) . . . let him be the first to throw a stone at her.'
- 'Why has the government taken this step against the advice of numerous experts on the subject . . . (pause) . . . because it is hypnotized by its own stubborn and unworkable policy.'

Here is how Lincoln used the pause to excellent effect.

> *My friends, it makes little difference, very little difference, whether Judge Douglas or myself is elected to the United*

> *States Senate; but the great issue which we have submitted to you is far above and beyond any personal interests or political fortunes of any man. And my friends, . . . (pause) . . . that issue will live and breathe and burn when the poor, feeble, stammering tongues of Judge Douglas and myself are silent in the grave.*

## FINALLY

The length to which you should hold the pause is difficult to judge or standardize. It requires experience, knowledge, and even instinct. It depends to some extent on the emotional content of the speech. To hold the pause successfully is a great thrill and achievement.

Leaders, thinkers, teachers, and writers understand the value and impact of the pause in speech. Charles de Gaulle, former president of France, tells us: 'Silence is the ultimate weapon of power.' The Dalai Lama, the spiritual leader of Tibetans, states: 'Sometimes one creates a dynamic impression by saying something, and sometimes one creates as significant an impression by remaining silent.' Mark Twain, the American novelist, notes: 'The right word may be effective, but no word was ever as effective as a rightly timed pause.'

# CHAPTER 30

## GESTURES

*Execute Gestures in the 'T' Zone*

Gestures are an important tool in a speaker's kit of effective communication. Humans have always used their hands and arms to communicate in addition to the spoken word. Gestures are an integral and indispensable element in how we communicate with our fellow humans. They enhance, support, and buttress verbal communication, and hence add tremendously to the overall impact of the speaker.

What to do with one's hands is always a speaker's dilemma. The answer is to execute gestures that are natural to you and that conform to your personality. They should be authentic to who you are. If you take up gestures that are not natural to you, or if you imitate someone else, you will come across as fake and insincere. In addition, you will be self-conscious and ill at ease, and hence will undercut your own effectiveness as a speaker.

Use hand gestures carefully, since too many of them can be distracting to the audience. Incessant, wild, and extravagant gestures are irritating and annoying.

Practise making full-arm gestures before a mirror until you have become accomplished in their execution. If you are speaking from behind a podium, it is all right to rest your arms lightly on the podium, which allows you to gesture freely. Do not lean with your full weight on the podium. If you are uncomfortable using your hands, drop them naturally to your side.

## AVOID THESE INAPPROPRIATE GESTURES OR HAND POSITIONS

- Jabbing the index finger at the audience. This is both condescending and aggressive.
- Gesturing first with one hand and one arm only and then using the other hand and arm. This is distracting.
- Gesturing solely with the arms, with the elbows clamped to the ribs. This is non-descriptive.
- Gesturing at the level of the thighs. This signals a lack of confidence.
- Gesturing with the fingers curled in and tightly clenched, with the thumb protruding. This signals hostility.
- Keeping the hands crossed across the chest or at the belt-buckle level or even lower. This signals defensiveness.
- Keeping both hands inside your trouser pockets (for men). This signals insecurity.
- Keeping the hands in the fig-leaf position. This signals defensiveness or vulnerability.
- Keeping your hands clasped behind your back. This just does not look right.
- Leaning back, with both hands supporting your head, when sitting. This signals a feeling of overconfidence or superiority.
- Steepling your fingers. This signals smugness or excessive self-confidence.
- Running your hand through your hair. This signals frustration.
- Tightly clenching or wringing your hands. This signals strain under pressure.
- Tapping your fingers or cracking your knuckles. This signals tension or nervousness.

- Fidgeting or tapping your fingers excessively. This signals nervousness.
- Chewing the end of a pen or pencil or biting your fingernails. This signals nervousness.

## THE 'T' ZONE

Gestures preferably should be performed in the 'T' zone or power zone. This zone extends vertically from above the navel to below the chin, and horizontally from the fingertips of your outstretched arms. If you were to gesture at the level of the thighs, this would be below the 'T' zone. If you were to raise your arms above your head, this would be above the 'T' zone. Follow these recommendations to make your gestures powerful without being distracting, effective without being annoying. *Execute gestures in the 'T' zone.*

## EXAMPLE FROM POLITICS

Adolf Hitler was a charismatic speaker who believed that leaders have to be actors. He studied the performances of a well-known comedian of his times to learn how to captivate his audience. As a political agitator in the early part of his life, he practised speaking to audiences as small as a dozen people and realized the importance of careful planning and preparation of material. In his earlier days, just like an actor, Hitler spent hours practising his poses and gestures in front of a mirror in his room. He continued doing this much later in his career, as photographic evidence shows. Hitler weaponized his hands, punching the air with his fist and wagging his finger, all choreographed to mesmerise his audience.

## CONCLUSION

Humans around the world, in all cultures and societies, and throughout the ages, have used hand gestures along with verbal language to communicate. Gestures show conviction and passion, indicating that the speaker believes in what he is saying. It is a declaration of the speaker's presence and a call for attention. Experts say that 65 per cent of the meaning that people take away from an exchange comes from the non-verbal. A study shows that the more popular speakers are those who use hand gestures twice as much as the least popular speakers. The speaker who gestures certainly appears more involved, more committed, more interested, more enthusiastic, and more expressive than the one who does not.

Every gesture adds to the picture, or overall optics, that the speaker is creating through his oral narrative. An important aspect is to keep the gestures in the area of the upper half of the body, considering your navel or belly button as the centre of your body. Your gestures should be in the zone above the navel and below the chin. If you want to harness the potential of gestures, identify the gestures you wish to incorporate into your speaking style and rehearse them in front of a mirror, just like actors do.

## FINALLY

Remember, hand gestures do not replace what you say. They emphasize and amplify what you say.

CHAPTER 31

# BODY LANGUAGE

## The Body Never Lies

Good speakers know that besides their verbal presentation, non-verbal communication is a critical element in getting across their message. They are adept at making non-verbal communication work for them in a positive manner. When you speak, you don't just speak with your mouth or through the words your utter, but you also communicate through your body language. This includes smile, posture, stance, choreography, eye contact, hand gestures, expressions, voice, and dress. They all add up to the body language that accompanies what you are saying (the words you are uttering) and that underlines your message and reinforces your style and method of communicating.

Body language is important in projecting an open, friendly, and positive image, a prerequisite for a powerful speaking style. The speaker's body language should convey confidence, ease, and self-assurance, and not arrogance, timidity, or defensiveness. Controlled body language can support your verbal message and reinforce your strengths as a speaker. Researchers in this area claim the importance of non-verbal communication as overwhelming. If this is indeed the case, you cannot ignore non-verbal communication if you want to be a truly effective and compelling communicator.

## ELIMINATE THE FROWN, DROP THE DEADPAN EXPRESSION

You should not be diffident or reserved. The stiff and remote speaker is not going to succeed. Aloofness and distance will alienate the audience. A wooden speaker who is undemonstrative will bore the audience and put them to sleep. If you are an impassive or poker-faced speaker, seek to drop the deadpan expression. Sometimes people deliberately prevent themselves from revealing their feelings for social and professional reasons. This includes the CEO who believes that showing a friendly face to colleagues compromises his authority; in certain societies, it is considered unmanly or unseemly to display emotions in public. However, on the podium, self-imposed reserve and restraint have no place.

On the podium, the speaker's face should reveal all the emotions in accordance with the context and content of the speech—seriousness, sincerity, determination, purpose, patience, forbearance, amusement, humour, frivolity, excitement, apprehension, and even anger. The audience should be able to read the emotions of the speaker from his facial expressions, and not merely judge them solely from the words being spoken.

An expression that I have found on many speakers is the frown. Many of us frown unintentionally when we speak. We do it as a matter of habit when we concentrate. This may be in reaction to a stressful situation. However, a frown is associated with disapproval and displeasure. It is threatening. It evokes negative emotions. If you are prone to frowning, then you must seek to eliminate this expression. One preventative is for you to practise before a mirror and break the habit of frowning.

## HERE ARE SOME TIPS FOR IMPROVING YOUR BODY LANGUAGE

- Smile naturally and frequently, using the smile as a powerful tool of communication.

- Adopt an erect and well-balanced stance.
- Take possession of your territory at the podium.
- Do not grip the podium with your hands as though holding on for dear life.
- Do not stand too rigidly at the podium.
- Use the space around the podium to your advantage, although do so sparingly.
- Execute hand gestures in the T zone or power zone.
- Establish eye contact.
- Make sure your face reveals all expressions and emotions honestly.
- Speak in a well-modulated voice.
- Sit or stand comfortably, with your shoulders back.
- Lean forward slightly.
- Do not frown.
- Do not slouch in your chair.
- Do not cross your arms.
- Do not cross your legs.
- Do not look down. Hold your head erect, at a natural angle.

Have a friend video record your next presentation and carefully analyse your body language—smile, posture, stance, choreography, eye contact, hand gestures, expressions, voice, and dress—and learn from it. Learn how to direct the orchestra of all these instruments, which add up to body language, so you can produce beautiful music, that is, a powerful speech.

## BODY LANGUAGE IN WILDLIFE PHOTOGRAPHY

When shooting wildlife, it is essential to understand and appreciate the body language of the subject in order to capture unusual animal behaviour and emotion. In order to increase the photographer's chances of doing so, it is extremely important to do research into the subject and to spend time getting to know the animal's behavioural traits. This will help the photographer to understand the animal better, to predict and anticipate what might happen, and to be ready to capture the *golden moment* whenever it occurs.

Just as the wildlife photographer attaches meaning and substance to the animal's behaviour as exhibited and amplified through body language, the audience attaches meaning and substance to the words uttered by the speaker and as exhibited and amplified through body language. Both the wildlife photographer and the speaker strive to achieve the golden moment when everything comes together naturally and effortlessly, when it all clicks together. And body language plays a key role in enabling this golden moment to take place.

## FINALLY

It is said that *the body never lies.* Remember the words of Peter Drucker, one of the most widely known and influential thinkers on management: 'The most important thing in communication is to hear what isn't being said.'

# CHAPTER 32

## PERSONALIZATION

*Personalize your Speech by using Personal Names*

If you include the personal names of certain individuals in your talk, you will ensure a high level of listenability and connectivity with your audience. When you tell stories, provide illustrations, or cite examples, always use specific names, unless it is a question of confidentiality or privacy. Personalization creates a sense of identity and empathy with the audience.

### DALE CARNEGIE

In his 1936 book on self-improvement, *How to Win Friends and Influence People*, the American writer Dale Carnegie writes: 'Remember that a person's name is to that person the sweetest and most important sound in any language.'

How true this is. Remembering a name and recalling it easily at the right moment is a most useful social skill. If you can do this smoothly and naturally, you will pay people you meet a subtle but effective compliment, a recognition of their individuality and personality, which they will greatly appreciate. People place an astonishing amount of importance on their own names.

One of the most important ways of gaining goodwill is by remembering names and making people feel important. As you walk into a room and are introduced to the people around, try to remember their names. If you do not hear properly the first time, ask for the name to be repeated. Try to associate the name with the person's features, expression, and general appearance. There are many techniques for remembering names and those who want to delve into this subject may read books on this topic.

## SOURCES OF NAMES

A good source of names to be used for personalization is the itinerary or programme for the conference, which will list the names of the chairman, co-speakers, and moderator. Another source is the people you are introduced to prior to the conference. Arrive early and make small talk with members of the audience and learn a few names as you go along. It is quite normal for speakers as soon as they arrive at the conference hall to be introduced by the organizers to various people as a matter of courtesy. These may be members of the audience or co-speakers. Try to remember their names as you go around and weave their names into your speech to ensure increased audience interest. Another way to find names for the purpose of personalization is to anticipate well before you arrive the people who are likely to be present at the event and thread their names into your speech.

## PERSONAL EXAMPLE

I was a director of Nestlé (India) Ltd. and a member of the audit committee for eight years, from 2011 to 2019. However, my professional relationship with Nestlé began in the early 1980s in my role as a statutory auditor and ended in 2008. I have fond memories of numerous Nestlé personalities and remember many interesting anecdotes stretching over a long period of nearly thirty-five years.

In my farewell speech to the directors and senior management of the company (Nestlé, Gurugram, 2019), I narrated interesting stories and anecdotes about Nestlé's history, along with specific names. I spoke about some of the fascinating personalities who I had met during my long association with the company. I also referred by name to the current managing director, Mr Suresh Narayanan, and to members of the audit committee, R.V. Kanoria and Dr Rakesh Mohan, who were present in the audience. In this farewell speech, I was specific and concrete, and personalized my anecdotes and stories with names and references to specific incidents, and this assured audience listenability.

## CONCLUSION

I always try to personalize my presentations by constantly referring to people in the audience by name. Single out people in the audience, or even the chairman or the co-speakers, and refer to them in your speech. This is a powerful technique for capturing the attention of the audience. If the audience is unknown, you can ask a member of the audience for his or her name and then address that person by name. This also enables you to establish eye contact with that person and with those around the person who you have singled out by name.

When giving a speech, even if you manage to remember a few names out of an audience of a hundred, and refer to those individuals by name, you will ensure audience awareness and listenability. *Personalize your speech by using personal names.*

CHAPTER 33

# HUMOUR AND WIT

Humour and Wit Break Barriers and Reduce Hostility

Every speaker has his own personality and I was always predisposed towards being the serious type. Humour and wit did not come naturally to me. Whereas there are other speakers with more bold, outgoing personalities for whom the use of humour is second nature. Be that as it may, humour and wit play an important role in making a speech interesting and pertinent, memorable and relevant.

There are subtle differences between humour and wit. Humour is the ability to amuse and make others laugh. Wit is more intellectual, biting, and insightful humour that can penetrate to deeper levels than the surface sparkle of a one-liner or wisecrack. It can cut the clutter and get to the heart of an issue. It includes acute observation, clever banter, and barbed comment. It can be cynical or insulting, which is what provides it with its characteristic sharpness. Wit can sometimes be cruel, inflicting wounds and deflating egos, so it needs to be used carefully and judiciously.

## ADVANTAGES OF USING HUMOUR AND WIT

*Humour and wit reduce hostility*, deflect criticism, and help in communicating difficult messages. Humour lowers defences, making audiences more receptive to your message and more supportive of your position. It also makes you more likable and approachable. The best humour is based on personal narrative. Humour does not necessarily have to elicit a hearty, loud laugh. It is good enough if you can make people smile or chuckle. The injection of humour is also a good point in a speech to reassess audience reaction and interest and to re-engage the wandering minds of some people.

## THE WIT AND WISDOM OF NANI PALKHIVALA

Nani Palkhivala, the eminent Indian jurist, used humour and wit so widely in his speeches and writings that after his death his scintillating remarks were compiled in a book titled *Wit & Wisdom of Nani A. Palkhivala*. Here are a few of his droll observations:

- 'To preach the virtue of stability to our Finance Ministry is like seeking to preach the value of peaceful coexistence to Genghis Khan.'
- 'Stability is anathema to the North Block.'
- 'The story goes that when other nations remonstrated with God that he had been very partial to India and had given it disproportionately large natural and human resources, God answered, 'To offset these benefits I shall give India—the Indian Government'.'

## THE WIT AND WISDOM OF RONALD REAGAN

Ronald Reagan, the former president of the United States, who was a Republican, was known for his witty remarks, making him one of America's most quotable presidents and winning him the epithet of the Great Communicator. Throughout his political career, Reagan used humour to win friends and influence voters. Some of Reagan's best observations are found in *The Wit & Wisdom of*

*Ronald Reagan,* compiled by James C. Humes, a former presidential speechwriter.

After surviving an assassination attempt in 1981, Reagan told his wife, Nancy, as he was being taken into surgery, 'Honey, I forgot to duck.' To surgeons, as he entered the operating room, he said, 'Please tell me you're Republicans.' During the 1984 presidential debates, when asked if, at the age of 73, he was too old to be president, Reagan said, referring to his much younger Democratic challenger, Walter Mondale, 'I will not make age an issue of this campaign. I am not going to exploit, for political purposes, my opponent's youth and inexperience.'

## THE WIT AND WISDOM OF KENNEDY

Kennedy was known for his witty remarks and snappy comebacks. His team kept a humour file in which they collected jokes from newspapers or from television for possible use in speeches. When travelling, an advance team would read local newspapers and talk to local people in search of locally oriented humour that would allow Kennedy to bond with the audience.

Kennedy's humour was subtle and self-deprecating. When a young boy asked him how he became a war hero, he responded disarmingly, 'It was absolutely involuntary. They sunk my boat.' No doubt there are many reasons for the enduring Kennedy legacy, but according to some his wit and humour account for much of his appeal.

## PERSONAL EXAMPLE

One of my best attempts at humour and wit was in my presentation to a delegation of French accountants visiting India (French Embassy, New Delhi, 1996). I understood the French character well, so I was able to build into my speech light-hearted comments about France, the French language, the French government, and

French companies that had made investments in India, which endeared me to the audience and won me repeated applause. I had analysed the speaking situation carefully. Though the topic was a serious one (accounting standards), the setting was not (the French accountants were on holiday in India with their spouses and attended the conference in casual dress after a shopping trip). My speech was lively and bright as demanded by the occasion and was well received. To have given it a business-like, serious tone would have been a disaster.

I introduced humorous asides and engaged in repartee. At one stage, I referred to the superb infrastructure in France and, leaning towards F. Alby, one of the organizers, asked softly, 'Why is there no French investment in infrastructure in India?' The speech was well suited to the moment. I had won over the audience and they were ready to applaud almost anything I said. I was able to connect with them because I understood the importance of humour, the significance of repartee, and the effect of riposte. I had slowly but surely built empathy and harmony with the audience. I reached out and connected with them and they reciprocated with applause. Later I received a very complimentary letter from Fabrice Adrian of the French Embassy stating that they 'highly appreciated the active fruitful participation' by both the audience and me.

## PERSONALLY

Many business presentations are full of facts and statistics, and hence tend to be dry and somewhat monotonous. Many of us who deal with facts all the time may find it difficult to include humour and wit in our presentations. I tackle this problem in a broader sense by identifying my weak areas, for example, regarding the use of humour, and consciously try to introduce some humour and wit in my speeches.

I work hard at overcoming my weaknesses as a speaker and to a large extent have managed to build into my speeches some humour to elicit laughs and chuckles from the audience. Sometimes I succeed and sometimes I don't. But I have realized that when I do include humour and wit, my speech becomes even more effective and people start liking me. Remember, once you can get people laughing, they will be listening and you can tell them almost anything.

## CONCLUSION

Do not adopt a serious or solemn tone throughout your speech. Create some lighter moments. Include some soft breaks. Work on these aspects during the preparation of your speech and mark in the prompt cards the places where you intend to use remarks or comments to shift the mood. If you can elicit chuckles, laughs, or claps three or four times during your presentation, you should be satisfied. You can narrate suitable stories, cite compelling examples, make interesting analogies, and use gripping metaphors. Analyse the nature and needs of the audience properly and you will find many ways of introducing humour and wit appropriate to the occasion.

## FINALLY

Let's remember Kennedy's advice: 'There are three things which are real—God, human folly, and laughter. The first two are beyond our comprehension, so we must do what we can with the third.'

CHAPTER 34

# FLEXIBILITY

Go with the Flow

Sometimes when you arrive at a speaking situation with a plan, as you must, it becomes difficult to suddenly adjust to changed circumstances and you may resist or object. However, inflexibility creates stress and is insensitive to the needs of other people, including your co-speakers and the audience. Learn to *go with the flow.*

## BE FLEXIBLE IN DEALING WITH SITUATIONS AS THEY ARISE

Plenty of situations will arise when your well-prepared and extensively rehearsed speech may need some tweaking or even major changes. You may have relied on one major instance or case study to illustrate your point of view and you suddenly find that another speaker before you has unwittingly usurped your example. What do you do? Should you stay with your original plan and repeat the same example? No, you should change gears and amend your presentation. But to do this, you must have reserve power. At the planning stage of your speech, you should prepare extra material that you may need to use if the situation so demands.

Sometimes a co-speaker may make a point that contradicts your point of view or gives a different slant to your argument.

What do you do? Should you cling to your plan? No, you should amplify and expand your argument even further by going deeper into the subject than you had originally intended in order to support your stance. But to do this you should have reserve power.

You should be flexible in dealing with unpredictable or difficult situations as they arise. Sometimes your place in the programme has a profound effect on what you say in your speech. If your talk is slated towards the end of the speaking event, you have to be realistic and acknowledge that others may cover what you would have said had you been placed first on the speaker's slot. In such situations, you will have to be flexible and accommodating.

## RESERVE POWER

Learn the art of carefully winnowing your final thoughts to only three or four. I may well start with a list of ten thoughts around the theme of my speech and finally, after extensive rehearsals, end up with only three or four. The remaining thoughts that have been jettisoned fall into the category of reserve power and may be plucked out of the discard bin whenever urgently required.

For example, you may have to answer an unanticipated question from the audience in the question and answer (Q&A) session following your speech. A pertinent question can sometimes lead you to explore new territory with your audience, and when you can, you should be flexible enough to shift gears to follow an interesting question or a thought-provoking line of inquiry. This is where the material you have discarded becomes useful and provides you reserve power.

## MIX AND MOVE AROUND

It surprises me to see how speakers fail to chat with their audience during coffee breaks and at mealtimes. I find these meetings, casual and brief though they may be, a source of material and inspiration for my speech and will often refer to a particular conversation with a member of the audience in my talk. For example, I might say, 'Someone was telling me during the break . . . and this leads to my next point.' This is an excellent way of getting your audience involved in the discussion. It shows them that you are approachable and accessible, friendly and open. It also benefits you because you are able to speak face to face with some members of the audience and learn about their interests and concerns.

## PERSONAL EXAMPLES

At a presentation on the energy and oil sector to the Central Board of Direct Taxes (CBDT, New Delhi, 1995), I faced many unknowns. I did not know who my co-speakers were going to be, what specific topics they were going to talk about, and the time and duration of my presentation. In view of these unknowns, I had to remain flexible in my presentation. Again, reserve power and flexibility enabled me to engage successfully with the audience. The steps that I finally took as I navigated my way through these unchartered waters were:

- I shortened my speech to fit into the time eventually allotted to me.
- I moved away somewhat from my prepared material because a previous speaker had touched on some points that I had originally intended to address.

At a presentation to a group of French accountants (French Embassy, New Delhi, 1996), I discovered that the accountants were accompanied by their spouses, that they were in casual attire, and that they had come straight from a shopping expedition as they were carrying many packages. I saw that they were in no mood for a highly technical presentation on Indian accounting standards. I immediately altered my presentation and included very few technical details. I made my speech light-hearted. I introduced humour. I introduced repartee. I improvised. I was flexible. Though I had come with a basic game plan, I read the situation quickly as I scanned the audience, and adjusted my strategy accordingly in order to come out ahead at the end of my speech.

## OTHER THINGS YOU SHOULD WATCH OUT FOR

- **Seating and room size:** Visit the venue beforehand, if feasible, to familiarize yourself with the arrangements. However, often this is not possible.
- **Speaking order:** The first or the last slot is preferable. The programme may or may not indicate this.
- **Stage:** Will there be a podium? Very often, you do not have a choice in the matter.
- **Microphone:** If the microphone is not a clip-on device but is the standard mic, keep it at chin height, about 6 inches away from your mouth.

## CONCLUSION

To be a more successful speaker, you must be flexible and yielding, not rigid and adamant. Accept the possibility that some parts of your speech may have to be changed at the last minute. If you make allowances for sudden changes in the schedule or other unforeseen events, then when this actually happens, you will not be flustered or overwhelmed or discombobulated. Train yourself to be flexible and accommodating. Build reserve power that will allow you to dig into material that you may have gathered but did not originally intend to use.

To be flexible and adaptable, you need to be a good listener. Listen to the chairman's introductions of all the speakers; listen to the co-speakers; listen to the chatter of multiple conversations around you. Listening will provide you the clues necessary for being flexible in your approach. Prioritize being flexible over being rigid. Make allowances for the inevitability of plans being changed at the last minute. This mental agility and accommodating attitude will help you cope with unforeseen changes and altered circumstances. When you are ready to go with the flow, you will be well prepared to handle most contingencies. You will not be upset or worried or confused. You will be more relaxed.

## FINALLY

Finagle's law of dynamic negatives, also known as Finagle's corollary to Murphy's law, states: 'Anything that can go wrong, will—at the worst possible moment.' Stay one step ahead of this law by learning the art of flexibility.

CHAPTER 35

# AVOIDING CRITICISM

*The Podium Must Remain the Highest Platform for the Discharge of Professional Obligations*

Never criticize. Even if the arrangements are not to your liking, even if the co-speakers have launched into a tirade or have made negative remarks about you in their speeches, even if your allotted speaking time has been cut short without sufficient notice, do not censure or castigate. Keep your cool and answer any questions that may be thrown at you in an entirely professional manner. Criticism and articulating your point of view even when it may contradict someone else's cherished belief are two different things.

## PERSONAL EXPERIENCE

Once I made the mistake of criticizing a co-speaker in a public forum and regretted it thereafter. It left a bad taste in the mouth and disturbed the mood of the audience, no matter how justified the criticism may have been. Thereafter, I resolved to never criticize anyone at a speaking event. Criticism solves nothing. It creates distrust, resentment, and anger. Taking a critical position extracts an enormous amount of energy and often alienates us from our co-speakers, and even the audience.

Instead develop tolerance, respect, and forbearance for different points of view, particularly at a public forum, particularly when you are giving a speech before an audience. Temper loses arguments and is counterproductive. Temper loses the audience and forfeits the goodwill and sympathy of listeners. Control and restraint are important.

## AUTOBIOGRAPHY OF BENJAMIN FRANKLIN

In his autobiography, Benjamin Franklin, the American statesman who played a major part in securing the independence of the United States and in drafting the constitution of the new nation, describes how he devised a plan of thirteen virtues for attaining personal moral perfection. He kept a small diary in which he marked by a little black spot every fault he had committed in respect of the thirteen virtues he hoped to cultivate. For instance, he made it a rule to forbear all direct contradiction to the sentiments of others and any positive assertion of his own. He forbade himself any word or expression that imported a fixed opinion and instead adopted expressions like 'it appears to me at present'.

He writes in his autobiography:

> When another asserted something that I thought an error, I denied myself the pleasure of contradicting him abruptly and of showing immediately some absurdity in his proposition; and in answering, I began by observing that in certain cases or circumstances his opinion would be right, but in the present case there *appeared* or *seemed* to me some difference, etc. I soon found the advantage of this change in my manner; the conversations I engaged in went on more pleasantly.

Benjamin Franklin attributes his remarkable success in public life to this 'art of virtue' in which he perfected himself. Three of his thirteen virtues will be of particular interest to speakers: sincerity, tranquility, and humility. Of sincerity he writes: 'Use no hurtful deceit; think innocently and justly; and, if you speak, speak accordingly.' Of tranquility he writes: 'Be not disturbed at trifles, or at accidents common or unavoidable.' Of humility he writes: 'Imitate Jesus and Socrates.'

Benjamin Franklin's advice to display the virtues of sincerity, tranquility, and humility and thereby never to lose your composure or end up criticizing others, whatever may be the provocation, should be well heeded by all speakers.

## THE PODIUM MUST REMAIN THE HIGHEST PLATFORM FOR THE DISCHARGE OF PROFESSIONAL OBLIGATIONS

It is necessary to show passion and commitment when you speak, but it is also necessary to subjugate and restrain your emotional reactions. Pitch everything you have into your performance as a speaker—gestures, voice modulation, eye contact, the lot. You may be tired after your performance, but you also need to be detached and dispassionate. Never rant from the podium. Erect a wall between your personal beliefs and emotions and your professional responsibility and official demeanour. People usually have strong views on religion or politics, money or morality, and sometimes you may be the target of personal, insensitive remarks that may exhaust your patience and tempt you to retaliate in a similar manner, but patient and detached you must remain. Never be provoked into a flash of anger by some nasty remark made deliberately. You are giving your point of view; others have the right to disagree. Do not get involved in heated arguments from the podium. *The podium must for you remain a place of decency and humility and the highest platform for the discharge of professional obligations.*

## FINALLY

Refrain from sarcasm, cynicism, rancour, derision, contempt, mockery, and invective when on the podium. Also, do not get rattled by hostility or animus, or allow yourself to become an emotional wreck and fall apart. After all, this is only a talk and not a matter of life and death. Try to maintain a professional detachment and equilibrium on the podium. Remember the counsel of Aldous Huxley, the well-known English writer and philosopher: 'There is only one corner of the universe you can be certain of improving, and that's your own self.'

CHAPTER 36

# EMPATHY AND HARMONY

*Build Soft Breaks and Lighter Moments into your Speech*

## LAUGHTER, CHUCKLES, EXCLAMATIONS, APPLAUSE, SMILES, AND NODS

Get to know your audience and build empathy and harmony with them, as I did on the occasions described below. Humorous remarks always ease the situation, creating a relaxed and friendly environment that helps you to communicate your message more coherently. *Build soft breaks and lighter moments into your speech.*

1. *French Embassy, New Delhi, 1996.* In a speech to French accountants, I talked about France, the French government, French investments in India, French GDP, and Peugeot, the popular French car company. Reference to things French helped create empathy with the audience. An observation of this kind invariably lightens the moment, generates laughter and smiles, and makes the audience more receptive to your main message.
2. *FICCI, United States, 1993.* In my speeches in the United States as part of the delegation from the Federation of Indian Chambers of Commerce and Industry, I compared the cost of household staff in India (in USD) as a fraction of the cost in the United States. The cost of household staff in India is very low because of lower wages and the lower cost of living. Comparing the figures in India with those

in the United States, where full-time household staff is a luxury only available to the affluent, led to exclamations of astonishment. Always give comparisons to something that the audience can relate to. I made the numbers meaningful by placing them in a context that the American audiences could connect with. By incorporating a soft break of this nature into your speech, you help break the ice and build affinity with the audience.

3. *All India Conference of Chartered Accountants, Hyderabad, 1993.* My audience analysis indicated that my audience would be chartered accountants, many from smaller cities. This was the unifying background. The conference was at Hyderabad, then the capital of Andhra Pradesh and now the capital of Telangana. I was delighted to address a large audience of nearly 800 people. I started by referring to the southern cities of Guntur (Andhra Pradesh) and Ernakulam (Kerala) which host a large number of small firms of chartered accountants. Since many of these accountants were attending the conference, they appreciated the reference to their hometowns and this initiated empathy with the audience. Making an observation of this kind—incorporating a local reference—always brings a smile and a cheer from the audience.
4. *South Asian Federation of Accountants (SAFA) Conference, Karachi, Pakistan, 1987.* In a speech in Pakistan, I identified myself with the foreign audience and praised the chairman of the host country, Mr E.S.H. Dahodwala. I wove his name into my speech and sensed the warm appreciation and friendliness of the audience that resulted from my doing so. The praising of a host country's chairman by a visiting speaker is always a good way of initiating harmony and establishing a bond. Mr Dahodwala became friendly, asked for a copy of my speech, shook my hand, congratulated me, and referred to me in his summary. Identifying with

the audience, together with humorous remarks and appreciative asides, always helps soften the moment.

## GOLDEN WORD 'YOU'

Persuasive speakers build empathy and harmony with the audience by using the golden word or power word 'you'. Pepper your talk with the word 'you'. Include sentences like 'Here is how you will benefit.' Use golden words like 'you', 'your', 'yours', 'yourself', 'yourselves'. Use 'we' or 'us' when you are part of the same group as your audience. Use 'I' when you discuss or refer to yourself, but use it sparingly.

## EXAMPLES FROM POLITICS

Both the prime ministers in the examples given below developed empathy and harmony with their respective audiences through the skilful use of the words 'you' and 'your'.

Here is how Boris Johnson, the British prime minister, highlighted the resolve of the British people during the Covid-19 epidemic in the United Kingdom (27 April 2020) through the use of these golden words: 'And thanks to **your** forbearance, **your** good sense, **your** altruism, **your** spirit of community—thanks to our collective national resolve, we are on the brink of achieving that first, clear mission . . .'

Here is how the Indian prime minister, Narendra D. Modi, in a letter to the people of India, which appeared in the editorial page of *The Economic Times* on 30 May 2020 under the heading 'Source of Strength is You', complimented the resolve of the Indian people in facing the Covid-19 pandemic. The letter contained the following sentences: 'There could be deficiencies in me but there is nothing that our country lacks. So, I believe in **you, your** strength and **your** abilities even more than I believe in myself. The source of strength for my resolve is **you**, **your** support, blessings and affection.'

Try to use the words 'you' and 'your' repeatedly in your speeches to build empathy and harmony with your audience. If you have prepared your speech well and succeed in establishing a warm and friendly bond with your audience, you can be confident that they will be open to your message.

## FINALLY

Sprinkle jokes, humorous remarks, or asides throughout your speech to create lighter moments. These softer moments will help you connect with the audience and engage with them better. These observations will make the audience like you and they will be more receptive to your message. Try to create opportunities for plenty of laughter, chuckles, exclamations, applause, smiles, and nods during your speech to build empathy and harmony with your audience. It is all about connecting with your listeners.

CHAPTER 37

# REACHING OUT AND CONNECTING

The Speaker uses all the Energy and Authority to Connect with the Audience

## COURT THE AUDIENCE

When next at a conference, you should analyse why some speakers are able to connect with the audience. Why is everyone listening attentively? Why are they engrossed in the talk? Why is nobody asleep, or looking out of the window, or trying to sneak out for an early coffee or tea break? The answer is because they are all hooked by the speaker's speaking style and personality, which compels the audience to listen to the talk and engage with the message.

*The speaker uses all the energy and authority to connect with the audience.* He reaches out to the audience through a combination of speaking techniques like balanced stance, eye contact, voice modulation, downward inflection, pause, hand gestures, and choreography. He targets the audience deliberately, wooing them with patience and concentration, courting them with focus and diligence, captivating them with carefully chosen words and phrases. Anyone who thinks it happens otherwise will end up giving dull, uninspiring speeches.

## DISPLAY CONFIDENCE AND AUTHORITY

I am surprised when some speakers start apologizing to the audience for something or the other. They apologize for various things: I am sorry I am late; I am sorry to take up your time; I am sorry I am unprepared. Do not apologize for anything (until you really are to blame). Do not offer apologies, excuses, or alibis. Do not hide behind innocuous, meaningless, empty words.

Instead, display your confidence and strength. Radiate authority and self-assurance. Be assertive without being aggressive, confident without being obnoxious, self-assured without being swaggering. Look and sound as if you mean business, and that you know your business.

Show your deep involvement with what you are saying. Physical involvement in delivering your message is important. It is important just as words are important. Stand still and do not fidget.

## STUDY THE VARIOUS STYLES OF OTHER SPEAKERS

At conferences, it is useful to study the various styles of other speakers. Try this experiment. Observe the strengths and weaknesses of speakers as they come and go and jot these in a notebook. You will find that compelling speakers have certain common attributes. Some will have an excellent balanced stance together with superb eye contact and expressive hand gestures. Others will have a smooth delivery and mellifluous voice. But what is certain to be common among all the good speakers is energy. They will inject every word and every gesture with energy.

Effective public speaking is hard physical work and nothing will happen if you do not put physical energy into it. You cannot hold the attention of your audience if you do not seem interested or involved in what you are saying. This is a two-way street. The speaker gives all his energy and authority in order to connect with his audience; the audience responds likewise by listening in pin-drop silence. Good speakers display energy and authority along with audience awareness.

## ESTABLISH 90 PER CENT COMMON GROUND WITH THE AUDIENCE

Reaching out to the audience requires *energy*, *authority*, and *audience awareness*, all conveyed primarily through body language and eye contact. The speaker begins his talk by seeking to establish some common ground with the audience; by the time he ends, he should have established 90 per cent common ground with them. Bonding with the audience is more than the sum of the individual speaking techniques and methods used.

When you reach out to your audience with energy and passion, they will feel the depth of your commitment and sincerity in such a manner that they too will reciprocate, giving you their undivided attention. The result of this two-way street—commitment by the speaker and attention by the audience—is a strong connection, an intimate feeling of sharing common ground. Both speaker and audience know instinctively when they have made the connection, and this strengthens their bond even further.

## HOW DO YOU KNOW?

You know if you have successfully connected with the audience by the reactions of people during the recess for tea or lunch after your speech. People will look at you with greater interest, establishing eye contact, or smiling or glancing or nodding at you. While some people will communicate their positive reactions or affirmations through body language, others will approach you directly for a personal chat or to compliment you. All these are explicit indicators that you have bonded with the audience. You know when you have made a great speech by the general mood of the audience. Ultimately, success is based on your bonding with the audience.

## PERSONAL EXAMPLE

One of my all-time favourite experiences is the presentation I gave at the first partners' conference (Deloitte, India Partners' Conference, Mumbai, 2004) after A.F. Ferguson & Co. (AFF) became a member firm of Deloitte, a large international accounting organization. The audience comprised all the partners of the legacy firms and many foreign delegates from member firms from around the world, many of them unknown to me. These were the challenges that I faced in establishing common ground.

Despite these hurdles, in my speech I conveyed energy, authority, and audience awareness through my style and used a variety of speaking techniques like:

- extempore speaking style but based on careful preparation
- balanced stance
- eye contact
- variation and modulation in voice
- pause
- examples and illustrations
- memorable moments
- dialogue
- personalization
- slides with minimum information
- flexibility

1. *Five essential methods.* I used five essential methods to reach out and connect with the audience. First, I used a delivery style that was seemingly extemporaneous but actually

involved considerable preparation, all of it supported by prompt cards. Second, I used a strong balanced stance and made eye contact. Third, I used personalization. In view of the large number of foreign delegates, I made it a point to refer to many of them by name and entered into a dialogue with some of them from the podium on a one-to-one basis. Fourth, I gave the audience two memorable moments: first, when I called up to the podium a member of the audience for three minutes to explain in detail a technical point; and second, when I paid tribute to, and called on the audience to applaud, a partner from the Canadian practice of Deloitte for his efforts in enabling AFF to become a member firm of Deloitte. Fifth, I used slides sparingly but effectively, and made sure they contained very little material initially. As I spoke, I introduced the rest of the material, mainly as 'pop-ups'.

2. *A touch of showmanship.* Through personalization and dialogue, I enhanced audience awareness and kept the audience hanging on to every word. When I chose a member of the audience to help me demonstrate a point or idea, I was rewarded by a noticeable increase in audience attention. This touch of showmanship helped in fully engrossing the audience in my speech. By making them a partner in my talk, I broke the barrier between listener and speaker.

3. *An intimate feeling of sharing.* I knew that I had reached out and connected with my audience of partners of all the legacy firms and foreign delegates because I received smiles, glances, handshakes, and applause after my presentation. The audience returned my commitment and involvement with their attention and pin-drop silence. The result was an intimate feeling of sharing. I reached out and bonded with my audience by essentially giving them a speech that was a combination of multisensory experiences.

I would not have achieved anywhere near this response had I just placidly (with no gestures and no expressions) read out my speech in a monotonous tone (with no voice variation), with my head buried in the script (with no audience awareness). Nothing would have happened. No bonding. No reaching out. No connection.

Never be boring or predictable or uninspiring. The secret weapon to being a good speaker is to capture—and hold—your audience's interest. As a speaker, you must be interesting, entertaining, compelling. Only then will you be regarded as a powerful and memorable speaker who has insightful things to say.

## FINALLY

The ability to reach out and connect with your audience can't be acquired overnight. It is driven, first of all, by the desire to become a better speaker. It takes hard work and endless practice. It may take years and many presentations before you master the art of public speaking.

Last but not least, remember that you will improve your ability to reach out and connect with the audience if you are able to weed out undesirable traits like arrogance, belligerence, sarcasm, and egotism. Instead cultivate honesty, sincerity, passion, and humility. Above all, convey humility of spirit through a pleasant disposition, patience, magnanimity, and the ability to laugh at yourself. Subjugate the ego to the message. These traits are worth acquiring if you want to become a compelling speaker.

CHAPTER 38

# TOTAL CONTROL

*The Complete Speaker Deals with Both Delivery and Content*

What do I mean by total control? If you have included or executed a majority of the techniques for power speaking in your presentation, as described in this book, you will gain a sense of total control. If you engage your audience through a variety of speaking techniques, and a bouquet of multisensory experiences, you will achieve total control over your speech and your audience.

## PERSONAL EXAMPLE

Let me give you an example where I achieved total control at a speaking event. I was requested by the Federation of Indian Chambers of Commerce and Industry (FICCI) to be part of a high-powered panel to make a presentation on the ease of doing business in India, to a business delegation from the Nanyang Technological University, Singapore (FICCI, New Delhi, 1994).

1. *A variety of techniques.* I used a combination of different tactics, as described below. All these are explained in detail in various chapters of this book.
    - extempore speaking style but based on careful preparation

- specifics
- slides
- picture words
- personalization, by referring to certain members of the delegation and to the co-panelists by name
- pause, followed by downward inflection
- rhetorical questions
- comparisons
- anaphora, antithesis, and asyndeton
- hyperbole
- breaks and recaps
- concluding summary

2. *Total control.* The financial newspaper *Business Standard* reported my presentation the next day and mentioned five out of the seven points that I had given in my speech. This was a compliment to me. I was quite surprised that the reporter had clearly understood the examples I had given in my speech. I realized that this was because of the methods I had used: structure, breaks and recaps, summary words, and rhetorical devices. It was a powerful reconfirmation to me that the techniques I was using were useful tools in making successful and compelling speeches. They resulted in my being in total control of the speaking event.
3. *Becoming a regular speaker addressing business delegations.* Two days later, I received a request from the FICCI secretariat to make a similar presentation to Japanese investors at an event hosted jointly by FICCI and another business chamber, the Associated Chambers of Commerce and Industry of India (ASSOCHAM). This was testimony that I had made my mark with my style of speaking with

FICCI and that they now considered me as a regular speaker to address foreign business delegations visiting India.

## ANOTHER PERSONAL EXAMPLE

Another instance of total control as a speaker was a presentation I made to the trustees of WWF-India (WWF-India, New Delhi, 1996), this time through the use of overhead transparencies and handouts. My presentation, incorporating many appropriate transparencies that had been created especially for the occasion, added a new dimension to the art of persuasion through visuals. The impact on the audience was gratifying. One trustee requested that all WWF-India presentations should follow the same template. Mr Samar Singh, the secretary general, said I should make a similar presentation to the staff. Mr S.P. Godrej, the president, requested a copy of the presentation for his company staff in Mumbai.

## A COMBINATION OF MANY TACTICS

Total control is achieved by employing a combination of tactics in your presentation at the same time. At times, the combination may change and the weightage of each technique may vary depending on different factors. Seek to give your audience a variety of multisensory experiences. It will be impossible for you to master and include all the techniques, which number more than fifty, mentioned in this book in any one speech. Aim for a judicious mix. The nature and scope of the mix will depend upon your analysis of the audience, but a solid grounding in the three fundamental pillars of speech making, namely a speaking style that appears extempore, filling your speech with specifics, and relentless practice, will help enormously. Add to these three pillars another five techniques: proper structure, balanced stance, sweeping eye contact, flexibility in voice, and rhetorical devices, and you have a winning combination. All these techniques are discussed in detail in separate chapters in this book.

Depending on the nature and extent of the unknowns in a speaking situation, you can employ other techniques like gestures, body language, and humour. Public speaking is very much like being the captain of a ship who has to keep changing tactics depending upon the roughness of the sea and variable weather conditions. Likewise, the speaker has to adopt different tactics for different audiences.

Keep in mind that people remember information when more than one sense is stimulated. Focus on the techniques relating to the auditory and visual senses. These are the two key areas that are essential for gaining total control over your speech as well as the audience: voice modulation, pace, phrase, and pause (auditory); and the stories you tell, the slides or photographs you use, and the picture words, body language, and gestures you employ (visual).

After each presentation, jot down the aspects of effective speaking that you handled particularly well and the aspects that you need to improve. This self-analysis and self-learning after the event will help you to work towards gaining and exercising more oratorical power in the next speaking situation.

## HOW DO YOU KNOW?

You know when you have achieved total control. You can recognize it after your presentation by the applause; by the nature of the questions you are asked; by the reaction of the audience; but primarily by your own sense of achievement. Aim for total mastery.

## FINALLY

The skilful and seasoned speaker will experience total control over all circumstances relating to the speaking event, from planning to delivery. Remember two words—delivery and content.

In another chapter, I mentioned the 80:20 ratio. The speaker should endeavour to spend 80 per cent of the time on delivery and 20 per cent on content. *The complete speaker deals with both delivery and content* and shines in both spheres, and by doing so brings the speaker and the audience together on a common ground, physically, intellectually, and emotionally.

Do not be in a rush. Build your reputation one speech at a time. Perfection is attained little by little.

CHAPTER 39

# IN THE EYE OF THE STORM

*Master the Art of Professional Detachment*

The eye of the storm is that one specific spot in the centre of a hurricane or tornado that is calm, almost isolated from the frenzied activity going on around it. Everything around the eye is turbulent, but the eye itself is still.

A lot of hectic activity goes on at conferences and other speaking engagements, before and even during the event. The organizers are busy making last-minute arrangements; the caterers are busy putting out the crockery for snacks and meals; the camera crew are busy with their lenses, camera stands, and flash; the co-speakers and the audience are busy networking. The representatives of the host organization are anxiously looking out for the arrival of the chief guest, hoping that he will be on time. If the chief guest is a politician or celebrity, there is even greater alarm if he is a few minutes late.

How gratifying and wonderful it would be if we could remain calm and serene in the midst of this human storm of ceaseless activity.

## AVOID ALL DISTRACTIONS

I once attended a speaking event in a small town where the standard for holding conferences was not high. On one side of the open hall, the caterers were setting up crockery and cutlery for lunch, creating quite a racket, even as the speakers were addressing the audience. The doors of the conference room were kept open throughout the event, allowing latecomers to stride right past the speaker's podium. Yet I remained calm because I realized there was no point in getting hassled or irritated. I could not fix the situation.

The arrangements at a conference may not be to your liking. You may be irked by poor stage management, lack of professionalism, and other disruptions. For example, at some speaking events, there are frequent interruptions, with people carrying papers, documents, or files back and forth behind the row of speakers lined up on stage, or people confidentially whispering into the ear of the chairman. All this can be disorderly, disturbing, and disconcerting not only for the speakers, but also for the audience.

Refrain from getting involved in such situations. Avoid all distractions. You have come to speak, not to supervise the conference arrangements. You must deal with the existing set-up the best you can. Despite various annoyances and vexations, you have to remain unruffled and serene. Certain things are not in your control, so it is best to accept the situation as it is. You must remain unaffected in the midst of this brewing storm.

## DO NOT GET CAUGHT UP IN THE STORM

As a speaker, commit to being calm and collected even in the midst of distraction and tumult. Practise listening. Practise breathing. Practise visualization. Let others be right. Avoid irrelevant debates or fruitless arguments. Do not get caught up in the storm. Be serene in the midst of all the activities related to the speaking occasion. The more composed you are, the more effective you will be when it is your turn to speak, despite the frenzy and often distracting activities around you. Cultivate professional detachment.

## EMULATE THE TRAITS OF THE PRAYING MANTIS

In the realm of animal symbolism, the praying mantis represents stillness, patience, and contemplation. After observing this creature for any length of time, you can see why. The insect gets its name because of the way it holds its two front legs, so it looks like it is holding its limbs in prayer. The praying mantis takes its time and lives its life at its own quiet pace. It remains still and only moves when it is entirely sure that it is the right thing for it to do. In many cultures, the stillness of the praying mantis is seen as evidence of the benefits of meditation and the importance of calming our minds. The message is to be still, to go deep within ourselves, to meditate, to cultivate quietness, and to seek a place of calm. With its forelegs folded as though in worship, the praying mantis symbolizes patience, stillness, quietness, meditativeness, and calmness. This is an ideal situation to be in for a speaker.

## PATIENCE MAKES YOU POWERFUL

When events do not unfold in accordance with our expectations, or when people do not behave as we want them to, we fall prey to negative emotions and often react without thinking. But if we think before we act, we can choose a response that determines the outcome. When we know how to wait and be still, we can choose the right path, overcoming adverse circumstances and obstacles till we reach our destination. Patience makes you powerful. We have much to learn from the praying mantis.

## PATIENCE IN WILDLIFE PHOTOGRAPHY

Most successful wildlife photographers know that patience—immense amounts of patience—is the secret to clicking the most unusual and interesting shots. If patience comes naturally to you, then you are lucky indeed. If not, you need to train yourself to be patient. Observing your subject and getting to know their behavioural characteristics requires patience. You may have to return to the area or habitat of the subject a few times to allow the subject to get used to your presence. Do not distract or frighten the animal, or do anything that will stress or spook it. Similarly, patience in public speaking can be a great virtue. Learn to deal with hostility; learn to deal with distraction; learn to deal with stress.

## PERSONAL EXAMPLE

In 1985, for five consecutive days, I was right in the middle of the storm, as I was one of the main witnesses to be examined on behalf of the defendants in the Tri-Sure India Ltd fraud case before the Bombay High Court. I watched with apprehension as the courtroom filled up with clerks, senior counsels, junior counsels, their supporting staff, other witnesses to be examined, and the public. I watched the arrival of Mr Atul Setalvad, the learned counsel appearing on behalf of the defendants, and the arrival of Mr Cooper, the learned counsel appearing on behalf of the plaintiffs. I looked with some apprehension at the wooden witness box, with its wooden railings, where I would soon be examined as a witness. This was a first-time event for me, something I had seen only in Hindi movies.

As the clock loudly struck the appointed hour, the courtroom rose to greet the presiding judge, the Honourable Justice M.L. Pendse. Eventually, I took my place in the witness box. I was young and as yet untutored in the art of relaxation techniques and public speaking. I was nervous and tense. I vowed that I would not allow myself to be exposed like this again. I would *master the art of professional detachment*, especially in a difficult and stressful situation. I would learn to live in the eye of the storm.

## FINALLY

I came to appreciate the virtues of patience and self-control, and the importance of going within and reaching a place of calm, much later in my life. These qualities are worth acquiring for the aspiring public speaker.

Part Three

# WORDS AND RHETORICAL DEVICES

# CHAPTER 40

## WORDS

*Use Words that Create Mental Pictures, Evoke Images, and Trigger the Imagination*

The public speaker must strive to develop sensitivity to words in all their forms and moods, and should dig deep within by using the right words for the right occasion if he is to reach the audience with his message. He must develop a large portfolio, vocabulary, or repertoire of common words and should learn to push harder to use the spoken word in all its forms: order, weight, colour, variety, inflection, pace, and phrasing.

### EVOCATIVE AND FACTUAL LANGUAGE

The English language falls into two main groups: evocative and factual.

The first is the language of the poet, the writer, and the orator. It is speech that appeals to the imagination, arouses one's sentiments, and evokes memories. It is the language of Shakespeare. Search for language that has emotional appeal. The best way of doing this is by reading poetry. The American poet, novelist, and playwright Paul Engle has rightly said: 'Poetry is ordinary language raised to the Nth power. Poetry is boned with ideas, nerved and blooded with emotions, all held together by the delicate, tough skin of words.'

The second is the language of the scientist, the accountant, and the engineer. It shuns emotion, is precise and matter-of-fact, and presents facts and data. Into this category fall the chairman's review of the annual performance of his company, the scientist's assessment of a new discovery, and the engineer's presentation of a blueprint for a new manufacturing plant. These reviews present facts coldly and objectively.

Accountants are generally more prone to making factual statements, whereas they need to learn how to use extra emotive, vivid, and graphic words so that they can become effective communicators. It is understandable, given their professional training and practice, that their natural tendency is to slant their words towards factual language, but it is important that they learn to enlarge their vocabulary so as to incorporate additional words that are expressive and that create pictures or images in the mind of the audience. The public speaker must learn to practise using both kinds of language—evocative and factual.

## PICTURE WORDS

Many speakers are not aware of the existence of *words that create mental pictures*. One way of defining picture words is a description that presents an object to the mind as if in a picture—one that is graphic, vivid, imaginative, creative, evocative, surprising, and even startling. Great picture words evoke images and feelings in the audience. The speaker who is easy to listen to, and one we long remember, is the one who sets images floating before our eyes.

Sprinkle words and phrases throughout your speech that create mental pictures and you will be more effective in reaching out to the audience. Learn to identify and deploy picture-building phrases. Use sentences full of concrete words and references to everyday objects like metals, chairs, tables, animals, men, and women. For instance, words and phrases like 'flooding waters', 'crashing wave', 'destructive hurricane', 'rustling leaves', and 'roaring crowds' create pictures in the mind. Stimulate the visual imagination of your listeners. Read Shakespeare to enhance your portfolio, vocabulary, or repertoire of such picture phrases. Use picture power. You will be more entertaining. You will be more memorable. You will be more influential. People buy more with their eyes than they do with their ears.

In addition to examples and illustrations, storytelling, analogies, similes, and metaphors, picture words are also powerful tools that help paint a picture in the mind of the audience. We remember pictures better than words. The more we use picture-oriented words and keep away from abstractions, the more we will be able to create visual images in the mind of the audience. We should do whatever it takes to help the audience remember what we say. If visual images and picture words arouse the senses, then we should sprinkle more of these in our speeches.

Churchill, during the darkest days of World War II, used powerful picture words and phrases like 'I have nothing to offer but blood, toil, tears and sweat' to rally the British people. Ronald Reagan spoke about the United States as 'the shining city upon the hill'. Martin Luther King, Jr. is remembered for his emotionally charged phrase 'I have a dream.' In each of these cases, the words used were concrete and not abstract, and conjured up word pictures of significant meaning. Train yourself to think and talk in terms of pictures, using similes, metaphors, analogies, or other picture words.

## EMOTIVE WORDS

Let me give you examples of the power of words that have survived long after the death of the speaker. These are the words of the poet, the writer, the orator, the statesman, the leader.

Lincoln in the Gettysburg Address in 1863:

- '. . . that this nation, under God, shall have a new birth of freedom and that government of the people, by the people, for the people, shall not perish from the earth.'

Churchill, in a radio broadcast to the nation in 1941, in answer to a letter sent by Franklin Delano Roosevelt, president of the United States, was at his most eloquent:

- 'We shall not fail or falter; we shall not weaken or tire. Neither the sudden shock of battle nor the long-drawn trials of vigilance and exertion will wear us down. Give us the tools and we will finish the job.'

Jawaharlal Nehru made this powerful statement at his trial for sedition in 1940:

- 'Seven times I have been tried and convicted by British authority in India, and many years of my life lie buried within prison walls. An eighth time or ninth, and a few more years, make little difference. But it is no small matter what happens to India and her millions of sons and daughters. That is the issue before me, and that ultimately is the issue before you, Sir.'

Jawaharlal Nehru delivered his famous 'Tryst with Destiny' speech in 1947:

- 'Long years ago, we made a tryst with destiny, and now the time comes when we shall redeem our pledge, not wholly or in full measure, but very substantially. At the stroke of the midnight hour, when the world sleeps, India will awake to life and freedom. A moment comes, which comes but rarely in history, when we step out from the old to the new, when an age ends, and when the soul of a nation, long suppressed, finds utterance.'

Jawaharlal Nehru in his eulogy for Mahatma Gandhi in 1948:

- 'In ages to come, centuries and maybe millennia after us, people will think of this generation when this man of god trod on earth and will think of us who, however small, could also follow his path and tread the holy ground where his feet had been. Let us be worthy of him.'

## ACTIVE VOICE

Use the active voice. Choosing the active voice instead of the passive voice is the most important step you can take towards delivering a powerful speech. The active voice relies on verbs. The passive voice is impersonal. Get rid of passive words and phrases like:

- is
- has been
- was
- would be
- would have been
- The mouse was eaten by the cat.

and replace them with active words or sentences like:

- The managing director inspected the department.
- You must make many decisions.
- The boy ran away.
- How to organize a meeting properly is important.
- The cat ate the mouse.

With the active voice, your content will sound more compelling, interesting, and animated. Another benefit of the active voice is that you will deliver your presentation with more emotion. Active-voice sentences simply sound better and are more likely to create images in the mind of the audience than the passive voice. With the active voice, you evoke emotion with your speech and your audience is much more likely to be persuaded.

## CHURCHILL AND THE 'SCAFFOLDING OF RHETORIC'

It is often said that a good speaker has a speech that is persuasive, possesses a musical quality, sustains audience attention, and embraces a wide vocabulary of common words so that all nuances of meaning are clearly defined and understood. Churchill was one such speaker. Churchill, when he was a young army officer in India, wrote an unpublished article called the 'Scaffolding of Rhetoric' in 1897, when he was still a very inexperienced speaker. It is astonishing to find that Churchill's love of rhetoric began when he was twenty-three years old and was in India. In this article, he noted the features that all great speeches and public speakers have in common:

- striking presence
- short homely words of common usage
- conversational style
- rhythm and cadence
- musical quality of words
- correctness of diction
- use of analogy

## USE SHORT HOMELY WORDS

As Churchill said in his article of 1897, it is best to employ short homely words of common usage. Use short words and phrases and simple direct language because this is how people talk. Use short sentences, simple, short, and common words, and direct, uncomplicated phrases. Language that gets right to the point is best. Do not try to impress your audience with your vocabulary of fancy words. Do not be ostentatious in your choice of words. Do not throw around sophisticated terminology and elaborate phraseology. Do not be rhetorically pompous. Use contractions. You use them in daily conversation, so why not use them when you speak to an audience?

Use words that bring you down to earth as a speaker and make you human in the eyes of your audience. Use a direct, conversational style. Picture yourself having a personal chat with your friends when you are relaxed and comfortable. Try to adopt the same easy and effortless style when speaking in public. Simple, terse, and to the point is always the best way to get your point across. This is what Churchill said: 'Broadly speaking, the short words are the best, and the old words best of all.'

## CARE ABOUT YOUR VOCABULARY

The speaker who cares about vocabulary will read as widely as possible and study the speeches of great orators and great authors and great playwrights. He will soon understand the importance of colourful words and compelling phrases. He will listen, note, and recall them and build a large portfolio of such words and phrases. No public speaker can hope to excel until he has acquired an extensive vocabulary and mastered it for his own use.

Strive diligently to increase and enrich your vocabulary. Reach beyond the confines of common conversational expressions and stock phrases, and instead gather into your kit a rich collection of words to express your thoughts. There have been some great communicators in history. They are remembered by their surnames: Lincoln, Churchill, Kennedy. It is not even necessary to mention their full names. It is natural that many of their quotations should appear in this book.

## BUILD A HOME REFERENCE LIBRARY

Build a collection of reference books that you can consult when preparing your speeches and presentations. Begin by acquiring the following books and get into the habit of referring to them often.

- Dictionary—a good up-to-date dictionary
- *Fowler's Modern English Usage*

- *Roget's Thesaurus of English Words and Phrases*
- A book of quotations—a good reference book
- *Lend Me Your Ears: Great Speeches in History* by William Safire
- The collected works of Shakespeare
- The Bible

## CONCLUSION

Use picture words, emotive words, musical words, and short homely words. Learn synonyms and expand your vocabulary. Use the active voice.

## FINALLY

We should always keep in mind this useful advice: 'Words can do more than convey policy. They can also convey and create a mood, an attitude, an atmosphere—or an awakening.'

CHAPTER 41

# RHETORICAL DEVICES

*The History of Rhetoric Dates back to Ancient Greece*

Learn how to use rhetorical devices to deliver your message in the most effective and impactful way. Rhetorical and other literary devices are figures of speech and persuasive strategies that elevate language and make it more engaging, memorable, and entertaining. When used properly, rhetoric can be a powerful tool for crafting speeches that stick in the mind of the audience.

A rhetorical device is a linguistic tool that employs a particular type of sentence structure, sound, or pattern of meaning in order to evoke a particular reaction from an audience. When carefully inserted, it can transform a speech into a memorable, evocative, and pleasant listening experience. It is due to these literary devices that the audience feels aligned to the speaker, and understands the uniqueness and depth of the text. Accountants, in particular, should expand their vocabulary so as to include the use of these rhetorical devices in their written and oral communication.

## RHETORICAL DEVICES

The roots of rhetoric go back to ancient Greece, so much of the terminology used to discuss it comes from the original Greek. Rhetoric, along with grammar and logic, is one of the three ancient arts of Western discourse. It was an essential element of classical Western education, especially in the training of statesmen, leaders, orators, lawyers, counsellors, historians, writers, and poets. Despite its ancient origins, however, rhetoric is as vital as ever and is used frequently by many skilled speakers and writers for persuading, informing, and motivating their audience.

Some common rhetorical devices are listed below. The first eleven have been described in detail in separate chapters in this book.

- *Antithesis* (which literally means opposite) is a rhetorical device in which two opposite ideas are put together in a sentence to achieve a contrasting effect. This contrast is apparent in the sayings 'Man proposes, god disposes' and 'Speech is silver, but silence is golden'.
- *Alliteration* is the repetition of two or more words that follow each other, or are placed close to each other in a series, having the same first consonant sound. It is the repetition of consonant sounds produced by the first letter of the words in the same line. Alliteration does not depend on letters, but on sounds. It makes for catchy phrases, memorable names, and pleasing sounds as seen in company names like Dunkin' Donuts, PayPal, and Coca-Cola.
- *Anaphora* ('the act of carrying back' in Greek) is the repetition of certain words or phrases, usually at the beginning of successive sentences, phrases, or clauses, to increase the power of a sentiment, or to convey and stress an idea. Here is an example of anaphora: 'Give me liberty or give me death.'
- *Repetition* is the simple repeating of a word or phrase within a short space in a sentence, with no particular placement of the word or phrase, to secure emphasis. Some common examples of repetition are 'boys will be boys', 'heart to heart', and 'home sweet home'.

- *Rhetorical question* is a question the speaker asks without expecting an answer. The idea is to emphasize a point, to encourage debate, and to prompt the audience to think beyond the obvious. Some examples are: 'Do pigs fly?' and 'Can we do better next time?'
- *Hypophora* is a question the speaker asks and then immediately provides the answer to it. This figure of speech is used to capture the interest of the audience, to create curiosity and interest, and to introduce a new topic of discussion.
- *Simile* is an explicit comparison between two essentially dissimilar things or concepts, usually using 'as' or 'like'. The two objects or ideas being compared are sufficiently different that any similarity between them seems unlikely. Some examples are 'cool as a cucumber', 'sly as a fox', and 'pretty as a picture'.
- *Metaphor* is a figure of speech in which an implied comparison is made between objects that are different in nature. It makes an implicit comparison without using 'as' or 'like'. 'Laughter is the best medicine' and 'time is money' are metaphors.
- *Asyndeton* (meaning 'unconnected' in Greek) is the removal of conjunctions like 'or', 'and', or 'but' because the sentence flows better, or more poetically, without them. A well-known example is 'I came, I saw, I conquered.'
- *Hyperbole* (from the Greek word meaning 'over-casting') is an exaggerated statement that conveys emotion, adds emphasis, and raises the bar for other speakers. It is not meant to be taken literally.
- *Litotes* is a figure of speech that employs an understatement by using double negatives. It uses negative wording or terms to make a positive statement or to express a positive sentiment. An example is 'The essay is not bad.'

- *Assonance* is the deliberate repetition of similar vowel sounds but in combination with different consonants in two or more words in proximity in a phrase or sentence. It is the repetition of internal vowel sounds in nearby words that do not end in the same way (e.g. *back* and *hat*). It also includes the use of identical consonants with different vowels (e.g. *killed, cold, culled*), or the use of the same consonants and different vowels (e.g. *hit* and *hat*).
- *Consonance* is an effective device of sound. It is repetitive sounds produced by consonants within a sentence or phrase. This repetition often takes place in quick succession (e.g. pitter, patter; slither and slather).
- *Chiasmus* is a technique wherein the order of two or more phrases or clauses in a sentence is inverted, but balanced, in order to create a powerful statement or effect. The best example comes from Kennedy's inaugural address in 1961: 'Ask not what your country can do for you—ask what you can do for your country.'
- *Parallelism* is a literary device in which parts of the sentence are grammatically the same, or are similar in construction. It can be a word, a phrase, or an entire sentence that is repeated. Martin Luther King, Jr.'s famous repetition of the phrase 'I have a dream' makes the speech compelling and rhythmic, as well as memorable. Parallelism can also be used to create a parallel position between opposite ideas through grammatical elements to order to emphasize contrast. This is seen in the astronaut Neil Armstrong's statement when he stepped on the moon: 'That's one small step for man, one giant leap for mankind.'

## CONCLUSION

In the subsequent chapters, my intention is to give you a basic knowledge of some rhetorical devices that are in common use, so that you can improve your ability to process and convey information while also strengthening your persuasive and communication skills. The methodology used by me is for the most part to give you many examples of each rhetorical device to explain its usage and meaning. These examples are taken from the speeches and writings of politicians, playwrights, poets, philosophers, jurists, and others, from ancient times to the present age, to make the meaning clearer. Enjoy the next few chapters on antithesis, alliteration, anaphora, asyndeton, and other rhetorical devices.

CHAPTER 42

# ANTITHESIS

*Contrasting Words or Phrases Pack a Punch*

Antithesis is the choice or arrangement of words or phrases that emphasize a contrast. Two ideas are expressed through the parallelism of strongly contrasted words. By focusing on contrasts, one idea is set or juxtaposed against another. Antithesis is a rhetorical device used by many orators.

Please note that the words used in antithesis in the examples given hereunder are words in common usage and not extravagant or unusual words. In the examples below, the strongly contrasted words are indicated in bold.

## EXAMPLES OF ANTITHESIS

Lincoln was a master at choosing words that emphasized a contrast:

- 'The world will little note, nor long **remember** what we say here, but it can never **forget** what they did here.'
- 'The brave men, **living** and **dead**, who struggled here, have consecrated it far above our poor power to **add or detract**.'
- 'With **malice** toward **none**, with **charity** for **all** . . .'

Churchill:

- 'Do not let us speak of darker days; let us speak rather of sterner days. These are not **dark** days: these are **great** days—the greatest days our country has ever lived . . .'
- 'You do your **worst** and we will do our **best.**'
- 'We know that he has, more than any other man, the gift of compressing the **largest** amount of words into the **smallest** amount of thought.'
- 'Never in the field of human conflict was so much owed by so **many** to so **few.**'

Martin Luther King, Jr.:

- 'I have a dream that my four little children will one day live in a nation where they will not be judged by the **colour** of their skin, but by the **content** of their character.'
- '**Injustice anywhere** is a threat to **justice everywhere.**'

Mahatma Gandhi:

- 'The **weak** can never forgive. Forgiveness is the attribute of the **strong**.'
- 'Live as if you were to **die** tomorrow. Learn as if you were to **live** forever.'

Jawaharlal Nehru:

- 'The children of **today** will make the India of **tomorrow.**'
- 'I have become a queer mixture of the **East** and the **West**, out of place **everywhere**, at home **nowhere.**'
- '**Great** causes and **little** men go ill together.'

Atal Bihari Vajpayee, former prime minister of India:

- '**Victory** and **defeat** are a part of life, which are to be viewed with equanimity.'

Benjamin Franklin, one of the Founding Fathers of the United States:

- '**Contentment** makes **poor** men **rich**. **Discontent** makes **rich** men **poor**.'

Henry Lee III, American politician, in a eulogy for George Washington, the first president of the United States:

- 'The purity of his **private** character gave effulgence to his **public** virtues.'

Richard Nixon, former president of the United States, in a eulogy for Senator Everett Dirksen of Illinois:

- 'As a man of politics, he knew both **victory** and **defeat**.'

Nani Palkhivala, an eminent Indian jurist:

- 'We have not **inherited** this earth from our **forefathers**; we have **borrowed** it from our **children**.'

Neil Armstrong, the first man to walk on the moon:

- 'That's one **small** step for man, one **giant** leap for mankind.'

Cicero, Roman senator in ancient Rome:

- 'For just as I approve of the **young man** in whom there is a touch of **age**, so I approve of the **old man** in whom there is some of the flavour of **youth**.'

Socrates, an ancient Greek philosopher, condemned to death, addresses his judges. It cannot get any better than this:

- 'But it is now time to depart—for me to **die,** for you to **live**. But which of us is going to a better state is unknown to everyone but God.'

## CONCLUSION

I thought the best way to explain antithesis is through examples. I have given you numerous examples of antithesis used by different speakers and writers over the ages. These examples from Lincoln, Churchill, Martin Luther King, Jr., Mahatma Gandhi, Jawaharlal Nehru, Atal Bihari Vajpayee, and many others show the diversity of speakers who have used this technique effectively and skilfully. If they can use it, so can you. I see no reason why you should not be using antithesis to express your thoughts in a speech. By focusing on contrasts, you are setting one idea against another. The words used in antithesis are familiar words in common use, and by no means effusive or exceptional or peculiar. I repeat, this is a rhetorical speaking device used by skilled speakers to make a particular point and ensure that it is long remembered by the audience.

CHAPTER 43

# ALLITERATION

*It is an Effective Device of Sound*

Alliteration is a rhetorical or literary device used to create or convey a message in a manner that is likely to be remembered by the audience. It is an effective device of sound. It is the occurrence of the same consonant letter or sound at the beginning of adjacent or closely connected words. Alliteration is used in a phrase or sentence beginning with or containing the same consonant letter or sound. Sounds, especially sounds in a sequence or series, make a strong impression and a speaker often uses alliteration to implant and reinforce a phrase in the minds of the audience.

In the examples below, the letters in bold represent the alliteration.

## EXAMPLES OF ALLITERATION

- **c**ool, **c**alm, and **c**ollected
- **l**ight and **l**earning
- **p**roximity to **p**ower
- **s**avage **s**pectacle
- **l**amp of **l**ife
- **m**onster **m**achines
- **t**ragedy and **t**rauma

## HERE ARE MORE EXAMPLES OF ALLITERATION

Lincoln:

- 'Four **s**core and **s**even years ago, our **f**athers brought **f**orth, on this continent, a new nation . . .'
- 'To care for him who shall have **b**orne the **b**attle and for his widow, and his orphan.'
- 'The South, flushed with **t**riumph and **t**empted to excesses; the North **b**etrayed, as they **b**elieve, **b**rooding on wrong and **b**urning for revenge.'

Churchill:

- 'The maxim of the **B**ritish people is **b**usiness as usual.'
- 'We shall not **f**ail or **f**alter; we shall not weaken or tire.'
- 'When we look back on all the perils through which we have passed and at the mighty foes that we have **l**aid **l**ow and all the **d**ark and **d**eadly **d**esigns that we have frustrated, why should we **f**ear **f**or our **f**uture?'

Kennedy:

- 'Let us go forth to **l**ead the **l**and we **l**ove . . .'
- '. . . race has no place in American **l**ife or **l**aw.'
- '. . . we shall **p**ay any **p**rice, **b**ear any **b**urden, . . . to assure the **s**urvival and the **s**uccess of liberty.'

Barack Obama, former president of the United States:

- 'They are part of the **f**inest **f**ighting **f**orce that the world has ever known. They have served tour after tour of duty in **d**istant, **d**ifferent, and **d**ifficult places.'

Sadhguru, Indian yogi and mystic:

- 'Bowing down to what seems powerful is natural. Bowing

down to what seems **w**eak and **w**orthless—that's great. That's devotion.'

## CONCLUSION

Alliteration is an oratorical and literary device that aids the audience in remembering the main points of the speech long after the event is over. Listeners and readers can remember these phrases because of the alliteration, which makes for a catchy, rhythmic, or lyrical pattern of sounds. The repetition of the same sounds at the beginning of a series of words can create a rhythm to the text, both when written and spoken. As such, these phrases reinforce the meaning and emphasize the main points.

I have given above examples of alliteration from different speakers from the past and the present to explain the meaning clearly. Again, note that the words used in these alliterations are words of common use and not exceptional words. Yet again, my list is dominated by Lincoln, Churchill, and Kennedy. Go ahead, enjoy yourself by using alliteration in your next speech and see how the rhythm of your speech improves.

CHAPTER 44

# ANAPHORA

*This is an Excellent and Indispensable Rhetorical Device*

Anaphora, a type of repetition, is an excellent public speaking device. It involves the repetition of the same word or words at the beginning of successive clauses or sentences. Anaphora is used as a rhetorical device to make and emphasize a particular point and is usually remembered by the audience because it sets up a repetitive pattern or pleasing rhythm to the speech. You can use anaphora frequently in a speech to move, motivate, impress, or connect with your listeners. In the examples below, the words in bold represent anaphora.

## EXAMPLES OF ANAPHORA

Lincoln:

- '**With** malice towards none, **with** charity for all, **with** firmness in the right . . .'
- 'But, in a larger sense, **we cannot** dedicate, **we cannot** consecrate, **we cannot** hallow this ground.'

Churchill during World War II:

- 'It is **victory**, **victory** at all costs, **victory** in spite of all terror, **victory,** however long and hard the road may be; for without **victory**, there is no survival.'

- '. . . **never give in, never give in**, never, never, never, never—in nothing, great or small, large or petty—**never give in** except to convictions of honour and good sense. **Never yield** to force; **never yield** to the apparently overwhelming might of the enemy.'

Kennedy:

- '**Let both sides** explore . . . **Let both sides** . . . formulate . . . **Let both sides** seek . . . **Let both sides** unite . . . **let both sides** join in . . .'

Jawaharlal Nehru:

- '**Peace is not** a relationship of nations. It is a condition of mind brought about by a serenity of soul. **Peace is not** merely the absence of war. It is also a state of mind.'

Jawaharlal Nehru's broadcast on All India Radio announcing the news of Mahatma Gandhi's assassination:

- '**All we know is that** there was glory and that it is no more. **All we know is that** for the moment there is darkness . . .'

Henry Lee III, an American politician, general, and statesman, in a eulogy for George Washington, the first president of the United States:

- '**First in** war, **first in** peace, and **first in** the hearts of his countrymen.'

Steve Jobs, co-founder of Apple Computers, in his keynote presentation on the iPhone used a combination of several anaphora. The simplicity of the common words used in this triple anaphora is quite stunning.

- 'In 1984, **we introduced** the Macintosh. **It didn't just change** Apple; **it changed** the whole computer industry. In 2001, **we introduced** the first iPod. **It didn't just**

**change** the way we all listen to music; **it changed** the entire music industry. Well, today, we are introducing three revolutionary products of this class.'

Jesus:

- '**Blessed** are the poor in spirit . . . **Blessed** are those who mourn . . . **Blessed** are the meek . . . **Blessed** are those who hunger and thirst . . . **Blessed** are the merciful . . . **Blessed** are the pure in heart . . . **Blessed** are the peacemakers . . .'

Old Irish blessing:

- '**May the** road rise up to meet you. M**ay the** wind be always at your back. **May the** sun shine warm upon your face; the rains fall soft upon your fields and until we meet again, **may** God hold you in the palm of His hand.'

I have kept till the last a very famous example of anaphora—one of the best—used by Churchill in his celebrated speech to the House of Commons during World War II:

- '**We shall** go to the end. **We shall fight** in France, **we shall fight** on the seas and oceans, **we shall fight** with growing confidence and growing strength in the air. **We shall fight** on the beaches, **we shall fight** on the landing grounds, **we shall fight** in the fields and in the streets, **we shall fight** in the hills, **we shall** never surrender.'

## CONCLUSION

Ne.xt time you are listening to a speaker, try to observe how many times he uses anaphora. Note down the actual words he uses as anaphora. This is one technique that orators down the ages have used most effectively. The repeated beginnings often lead to an active parallel construction of sentences. Anaphora need not be restricted for use only by politicians. It can be used very smartly by you as well. You need to design your own anaphora early on when you start gathering the material for your speech or presentation. It can be a combination of words appearing at the beginning of successive sentences or after a gap later in the paragraph. It works. It excites. It persuades. It motivates.

CHAPTER 45

# REPETITION

*Repetition is the Best Rhetoric*

There is an old Chinese saying that each **generation** builds a **road** for the next. The **road** has been well built for us, and I believe it incumbent upon us, in our **generation**, this year of 1962, to build our **road** for the next **generation**.

In the above example taken from a speech by Kennedy, the words *road* and *generation* are repeated to provide a harmonious integration of thought.

Repetition is another powerful speaking device as it can drive home an idea, underline an argument, and emphasize a point. Words used in repetition should be similar in application and not dissimilar. The word being repeated should not be used in proximity with the word being used or applied in a different way or with a different meaning. The sense in which the repeated word is used should echo the meaning of the word when it is used first. In the examples above and below, the words used in repetition are indicated in bold.

## EXAMPLES OF REPETITION

Lincoln:

- 'But in the right to eat the bread, without leave of anybody else, which his own hand earns, he is my **equal,** and the

**equal** of Judge Douglas, and the **equal** of every living man.'

- 'The dogmas of the quiet past are inadequate to the stormy present. The **occasion** is piled high with difficulty, and we must rise with the **occasion**. As our case is **new**, so we must think **anew** and act **anew**.'
- 'You may **fool** all the people some of the time; you can even fool some of the people all the time, but you can't **fool** all of the people all the time.'

Kennedy:

- 'Now the trumpet summons us again—not as a **call** to bear arms, though arms we need; not as a **call** to battle, though embattled we are—but a **call** to bear the burden of a long twilight struggle, year in and year out . . .'

Mahatma Gandhi:

- 'Religions are **different roads** converging upon the same point. What does it matter that we take **different roads,** so long as we reach the same goal?'

Jawaharlal Nehru:

- 'Time is not measured by the passing of years, but by **what one** does, **what one** feels, and **what one** achieves.'

Atal Bihari Vajpayee, former prime minister of India:

- 'If **India** is not secular, then **India** is not **India** at all.'
- '**Empowering** the individual means **empowering** the nation. And empowerment is best served through **rapid** economic growth with **rapid** social change.'

Sadhguru, an Indian yogi and mystic:

- 'Do not try to be the **best**, just do your **best**.'

Robert Frost, famous American poet, used repetition which is also an anaphora:

- 'The woods are lovely, dark and deep, but I have promises to keep, **and miles to go before I sleep, and miles to go before I sleep**.'

Shakespeare in 'Julius Caesar':

- 'I will not do them **wrong**; I rather choose to **wrong** the dead, to **wrong** myself and you, than I will **wrong** such honourable men.' (Marc Antony, Act 3, Scene 2)
- 'We all stand up against the **spirit** of **Caesar**, and in the **spirit** of men there is no blood; O that we then could come by **Caesar's** spirit, and not dismember **Caesar!**' (Brutus, Act 2, Scene 1)

Saint Thiruvalluvar, a celebrated Tamil poet and philosopher, who is said to have lived more than 2,000 years ago, used repetition:

- 'Fate's **strength**, one's **strength**, the adversary's **strength**, allies' **strength**, weigh all these and decide your course of action.'

The incorrect way to use repetition is as follows. This is a haphazard repetition of the word *association* having two different meanings and will not work.

- 'Sir William White has now received the crowning distinction of the Presidency of the Royal **Association**; his **association** with the Navy may be said to date almost from his birth.'

## CONCLUSION

I have given you examples of repetition used by Lincoln, Kennedy, Jawaharlal Nehru, Atal Bihari Vajpayee, Saint Thiruvalluvar, and others through the ages. Do you see from these examples how effective repetition can be? The repetitive words used in the above examples like *equal, best, sleep, wrong, spirit, strength* are all simple words of common usage. You can benefit from the use of repetition for emphasis in your presentations. Try it next time and see how you feel about it. It will add a little extra zing to your speeches.

CHAPTER 46

# RHETORICAL QUESTION AND HYPOPHORA

*These Oratorical Devices are Excellent Ways of Ensuring Audience Involvement*

A rhetorical question is a question asked by the speaker without expecting an answer. The question might not have an answer, or it might have an obvious answer. A rhetorical question is an oratorical device and a fantastic way to get the audience involved in the discussion. From ancient times to the present, orators have put their points of view across by asking rhetorical questions whose implied answers clearly support their views.

Hypophora, on the other hand, is where the speaker poses a question and then answers it immediately, that is, the speaker himself answers the question just raised by him.

The two oratorical devices, rhetorical question and hypophora, are sometimes confused, but there is a clear difference. In the first, the answer is implied or no answer is given by the speaker; in the second, an answer is provided by the speaker.

## EXAMPLES OF RHETORICAL QUESTION (THE ANSWER IS IMPLIED OR NO ANSWER IS GIVEN)

Ronald Reagan, former president of the United States, used a series of rhetorical questions, referred to as 'stacked' rhetorical questions, in his nomination acceptance speech at the Republican

National Convention:

- 'Can anyone look at the record of this administration and say, "Well done"? Can anyone compare the state of our economy when the Carter Administration took office with where we are today and say, "Keep up the good work"? Can anyone look at our reduced standing in the world today and say, "Let's have four more years of this"?'

Bill Clinton, former president of the United States, in his second inaugural address:

- 'The challenge of our past remains the challenge of our future: Will we be one nation, one people, with one common destiny, or not? Will we all come together, or come apart?'

Hillary Clinton, an American politician, accepting the Democratic Party's 2016 presidential nomination, in her speech to the Democratic National Convention:

- 'A president should respect the men and women who risk their lives to serve our country, including Captain Khan and the sons of Tim Kaine and Mike Pence, both Marines. So just ask yourself: Do you really think Donald Trump has the temperament to be commander-in-chief?'

Shakespeare in 'Julius Caesar':
Rhetorical question by Marc Antony, Act III, Scene 1:

- 'O mighty Caesar! dost thou lie so low? Are all thy conquests, glories, triumphs, spoils, Shrunk to this little measure?'

## EXAMPLES OF HYPOPHORA (THE ANSWER IS PROVIDED BY THE SPEAKER)

Here is how Churchill used this rhetorical device very effectively in one of his famous perorations during World War II, to the House of Commons:

- 'You ask, what is our policy? I will say: It is to wage war, by sea, land and air, with all our might and with all the strength that God can give us; . . . You ask, what is our aim? I can answer in one word: victory; victory at all costs, victory in spite of all terror, victory, however long and hard the road may be; for without victory, there is no survival.'

Dwight D. Eisenhower, former president of the United States, in his 'I shall go to Korea' address:

- 'When the enemy struck on that June day of 1950, what did America do? It did what it always has done in all its times of peril. It appealed to the heroism of its youth.'

Shakespeare in 'Julius Caesar':
Rhetorical question by Brutus, Act 1: Scene 2:

- 'What means this shouting? I do fear the people Choose Caesar for their king.'

Shakespeare in 'Merchant of Venice':
Rhetorical question by Shylock, Act 3, Scene 1:

- 'If you prick us, do we not bleed? If you tickle us, do we not laugh? If you poison us, do we not die? And if you wrong us, shall we not revenge?'

## CONCLUSION

Sometimes rhetorical questions and hypophora are deployed to punch up a point. If the answer is glaringly obvious, it will make that answer stand out even more. Sometimes these oratorical devices are used to persuade, convince, or win over the listener. You may be wondering when to ask a rhetorical question or employ hypophora. Typically, they are used in conversations where the speaker wants to drive an important point home. Making your point in the form of a rhetorical question or using hypophora is sometimes more striking, more effective, and more useful than making a flat statement or bland assertion.

# CHAPTER 47

## SIMILE AND METAPHOR

*Men of Straw*

A simile is a comparison of one thing to another. It describes a person, object, or idea by referring to something that is considered to possess similar characteristics or traits. The simile is known by the use of 'as' or 'like' or other announcement of conscious comparison. It is a more direct, less subtle version of a metaphor.

Metaphors are a time-honoured way of explaining the abstract in a more understandable, interesting, and arresting fashion.

The essence of a metaphor is understanding one kind of thing or experience in terms of another. For instance, the phrase 'he is a lion in battle' transfers the qualities of a lion, namely ferocity and courage, to a person.

There are many kinds of metaphors. Allegory, anecdote, proverb, parable, and fairy tale are examples of different types of metaphors.

Similes and metaphors are often confused, but they are quite different. As noted above, a simile uses the words 'as' and 'like' to draw a comparison, while a metaphor simply states the comparison without using the words 'as' and 'like'. The simile makes a direct and explicit comparison while the metaphor makes an indirect, implied, or implicit comparison.

## EXAMPLES OF SIMILE

- power is poison
- men of straw
- as hard as a rock
- heart of stone
- as bold as brass
- as innocent as a lamb
- as sweet as sugar
- as light as a feather

## EXAMPLES OF METAPHOR

- Greed rears its ugly head.
- He has an ego large enough to block out the sun.
- It is like walking a tightrope without a net.
- It never rains but it pours.
- Broken eggs cannot be mended.
- In the Middle East, peace is like finding a spring in the desert.

Lincoln

- 'It is an old and true maxim that 'a drop of honey catches more flies than a gallon of gall'.'

Churchill

- 'From Stettin in the Baltic to Trieste in the Adriatic, an iron curtain has descended across the Continent.'

Mahatma Gandhi

- 'I will not let anyone walk through my mind with their dirty feet.'

Douglas MacArthur, a retired United States army general, in his farewell speech used an appropriately military, if melancholy, metaphor:

- 'In my dreams I hear again the crash of guns, the rattle of musketry, the strange, mournful mutter of the battlefields.'

Benjamin Disraeli, former British prime minister, described the ministers on the Treasury Bench in the House of Commons with a striking metaphor:

- 'You behold a range of exhausted volcanoes. Not a flame flickers on a single pallid crest. But the situation is still dangerous. There are occasional earthquakes, and ever and anon the dark rumbling of the sea.'

Napoleon Bonaparte used a food or culinary metaphor to argue that soldiers, workers, and others cannot perform their duty properly unless they are well fed:

- 'An army marches on its stomach.'

Salman Rushdie, author, in a speech at a university used a metaphor to describe his life of isolation and hiding under a death threat:

- 'I have now spent over a thousand days in just such a balloon . . .'

Among the many figures of speech used by Jesus in the Sermon on the Mount, foremost is the metaphor:

- 'Ye are the salt of the earth.'
- 'Ye are the light of the world.'
- 'A city that is set on a hill cannot be hid.'

## CONCLUSION

Similes and metaphors are dynamic ways of creating picture words in the mind of the audience. Believe me, they will be remembered much more readily than abstract words. Look for or create interesting metaphors to use in your speeches and you will not only build the audience's interest but also stimulate their imagination. Note how striking and vivid is Mahatma Gandhi's metaphor, 'I will not let anyone walk through my mind with their dirty feet.' However, metaphors should be used sparingly. They can be formidable devices of persuasion.

CHAPTER 48

# ANIMAL SIMILES AND METAPHORS

*The Elephant in the Room*

Our language is replete with powerful animal similes and metaphors which can often convey meaning in a direct and clear-cut manner. Let us examine some of these.

## EXAMPLES OF ANIMAL SIMILES AND METAPHORS

- she is no spring chicken
- sly as a fox
- snake in the grass
- a leopard never changes its spots
- he is a night owl
- paper tiger
- black sheep
- cash cow
- putting the cart before the horse
- lone wolf

## HERE ARE MORE EXAMPLES OF ANIMAL SIMILES AND METAPHORS

Churchill:

- 'An appeaser is one who feeds a crocodile—hoping it will eat him last.'

- 'Dictators ride to and fro upon tigers from which they dare not dismount. And the tigers are getting hungry.'

Kennedy:

- 'Khrushchev reminds me of the tiger hunter who has picked a place on the wall to hang the tiger's skin long before he has caught the tiger. This tiger has other ideas.'

Franklin Delano Roosevelt, former president of the United States, in his fireside chat to the nation authorized US warships to fire first against Nazi naval vessels, which he called 'the rattlesnakes of the Atlantic':

- 'But when you see a rattlesnake poised to strike, you do not wait until he has struck before you crush him.'

Boris Yeltsin, former president of the Russian Federation, used this powerful figure of speech to describe certain fallen-out coup leaders:

- 'Like cockroaches in a bottle, trying to eat each other.'

P. Chidambaram, former finance minister of India, commenting on the country's economic condition said in a tweet:

- 'No wonder, the government is like a deer caught between the highlights—paralysed and unable to move in either direction.'

## LINCOLN AND ANIMAL METAPHORS

What strikes any student of Lincoln's speeches and writings is his frequent use of images and figurative language. His speeches and letters abound with metaphors. Many of them are extraordinarily well chosen and have the persuasive power of concreteness and clarity. Lincoln's success as a communicator lay in his skill in the use of figurative language of which the metaphor is the most common example. He used 'live' metaphors to illustrate complex ideas and to simplify abstract concepts, thereby giving life and meaning to something that might otherwise escape comprehension. Lincoln was particularly fond of animal metaphors and used them widely and effectively.

- 'Hold on with a bulldog grip, and chew and choke as much as possible.'

When, during the American Civil War, a commander boasted that he had built the 'finest army on the planet', Lincoln replied:

- 'The hen is the wisest of all the animal creation because she never cackles until the egg is laid.'

Lincoln described a certain situation during the American Civil War in this fashion:

- 'Grant [General Ulysses S. Grant] has the bear by the hind leg while Sherman [General William T. Sherman] takes off the hide.'

In a dispatch to one of his commanders, Lincoln wrote:

- 'In one word, I would not take any risk of being entangled upon the river, like an ox jumped half over a fence, and liable to be torn by dogs, front and rear, without a fair chance to gore one way or kick the other.'

## CONCLUSION

Metaphors, particularly animal metaphors, are an excellent way to explain things. We tend to understand and remember metaphorical language more easily as it activates our imagination and triggers our mental imagery. Metaphors that are graphic, arresting, creative, evocative, and startling let your audience process ideas in two channels of the brain, creating a deeper impact as they sync the visual with the verbal. See how clear, simple, and informative Lincoln's animal metaphor is: 'The hen is the wisest of all the animal creation because she never cackles until the egg is laid.' Learning to express your thoughts through metaphors adds some sparkle to your speech, besides stimulating mental images among the listeners.

CHAPTER 49

# ASYNDETON

*This is the Omission of Most Coupling Words*

Asyndeton is the omission of most coupling words or conjunctions like 'and', 'or', 'but', 'for', 'nor', 'so', and 'yet', to show insistency, to help increase the tempo of the sentence, and to highlight a specific idea.

Asyndeton, meaning unconnected, is the deliberate omission for dramatic effect of conjunctions by which a series of related words, phrases, clauses, or sentences in normal speech are connected. The staccato effect is thought to introduce some kind of liveliness. Staccato means to detach and describes anything that is made, done, or happens in an abrupt or disjointed way.

This rhetorical device is used by speakers to achieve a specific effect so that their messages can be remembered by audiences. It is to be used sparingly. The Greek philosopher Aristotle said that asyndeton is more effective in oratory than in writing.

The words or phrases used in asyndeton are indicated in italics below.

## EXAMPLES OF ASYNDETON

- *Lectureships, television, journalism* are kinds of jobs that command respect.
- Manchester has a tradition of *fine journalism, fine libraries, fine music.*

- He was *a bag of bones, a floppy doll, a broken stick, a maniac.*

Here are more examples of asyndeton:
Lincoln:

- '. . . that government *of the people, by the people, for the people,* shall not perish from the earth.'

Churchill:

- '*Forward, unflinching, unswerving, indomitable,* till the whole task is done and the whole world is safe and clean.'
- 'In his prime, Sir, *his power, his influence, his initiative* was unequalled in the land.'
- 'All is over. *Silent, mournful, abandoned, broken,* Czechoslovakia recedes into the darkness.'
- 'Meanwhile, *never flinch, never weary, never despair.*'

Kennedy:

- 'Let every nation know, whether it wishes us well or ill, that we shall *pay any price, bear any burden, meet any hardship, support any friend, oppose any foe* to assure the survival and the success of liberty.'

Steve Jobs, co-founder, Apple Computers:

- 'Let's take a look at the side. It's really thin. It's thinner than any smart phone out there, at 11.6 millimeters. *Thinner than the Q, thinner than the BlackJack, thinner than all of them.*'

Julius Caesar:

- 'I came, I saw, I conquered.'

Saint Paul the Apostle:

- '*I have fought the good fight, I have finished the course, I have kept the faith.*'

## CONCLUSION

Rhetorical devices like asyndeton are too often cast as the province of the great Roman orators. They shouldn't be. Out of the examples given above, my favourite is the last one, by Saint Paul, where the staccato effect is dramatic: 'I have fought the good fight, I have finished the course, I have kept the faith.' When executed well, asyndeton can spice up your speeches, presentations, even your one-on-one conversations.

CHAPTER 50

# HYPERBOLE AND LITOTES

*Here are Two more Rhetorical Devices to Liven up Your Speech*

## HYPERBOLE

Hyperbole is the use of exaggeration for emphasis in speech or rhetoric. It is an exaggerated, overblown, or extravagant statement, assertion, or claim not meant to be taken literally. The aim is to create an effect or to drive home a point in a dramatic or memorable way.

Here are some examples of hyperbole, indicated in bold:

- He stood **tall as a mountain.**
- He could **sell refrigerators to Eskimos.**
- A **thousand apologies** for being late.
- Events are moving at **lightning speed**.
- The bag **weighed a ton.**
- I was so hungry I could **eat a horse!**
- I could **sleep for a year,** I was so tired.
- I've **told you a million times** to help with the housework.

## LITOTES

Litotes is the opposite of hyperbole. Litotes is essentially a double negative. It is a figure of speech consisting of an understatement in which an affirmative is expressed by negating its opposite. It is the use of a negative statement in order to emphasize a positive meaning, in an ironic and deliberate way. Litotes is a common literary device used in speech, rhetoric, and non-fiction. It prompts the listener or reader to carefully consider what is being said and ponder the actual meaning of the statement.

Here are some examples of litotes, indicated in bold:

- The food is **not bad** (instead of good)
- This point is **not to be overlooked** (instead of important)
- She's **no dummy** (instead of smart)
- This is **no small problem** (instead of a big problem)

Part Four

# SELF-ANALYSIS

# CHAPTER 51

## FEEDBACK

*It can Reinforce your Speaking Style*

Feedback is an essential part of learning. Always look for feedback. If it is positive, it will boost your confidence and provide affirmation that your speaking style is effective in connecting with your audience. Additionally, it will provide answers to the questions about where, when, and how you should tweak your speaking style in order to be an even more influential speaker. Let me be clear—no member of the audience is likely to walk up to you after your speech and tell you to your face that it was a very boring speech. But they are likely to reveal their feelings through verbal (comments, questions) or non-verbal communication (gestures, body language), whether they thought the speech was interesting or dull. As a speaker, you need to learn to pick up these signals given by your audience after your speech.

### PERSONAL EXAMPLES

1. *Indian Oil Executives.* In 1995, I made a presentation on 'Accounting Standards' to the executives of Indian Oil (ICAI, New Delhi, 1995). Eleven years later, in 2006, I met an accountant who had been a part of the audience; he complimented me on the presentation I had made. This was one of the best compliments that I have ever received.

I just found it amazing—a speech being remembered after eleven years!

2. *Institute of Internal Auditors.* Some years after my speech on 'Be Effective or Bust' at a conference organized by the Institute of Internal Auditors (IIA, New Delhi, 1997), I met a person who had heard me and who remembered a particular slide out of the numerous slides that I had presented. This reinforced to me that my policy of adhering to a few main points, supported with suitable examples and illustrations, was the correct way forward. Such affirmation and appreciation of my speaking style strengthened my belief that my overall approach was appropriate.
3. *Assessing Opportunities in India.* I visited Dubai to make a presentation on 'Assessing Opportunities in India' (Dubai, 1994). I used many of the techniques discussed in this book: structure, balanced stance, eye contact, voice modulation, and body language in my speech. Some of my best presentations have been those where I have spoken from a mental outline supported by prompt cards and further backed by hours of practice. I seldom speak without practice. Many in the audience complimented me on communicating a precise and clear message. The Indian ambassador to Kuwait requested me to make a similar presentation in Kuwait.

## MINGLE WITH THE AUDIENCE

Mingle with the crowd after your presentation and solicit feedback about your speech. Not receiving any feedback is bad news, as it means that you have made little impact and indicates that you need to make changes to your speaking style if you wish to connect with your audience. During the interval after your speech, you will know soon enough whether you have connected with your audience.

This was brought home to me most significantly when I was speaking to an audience of over 800 people at the 13th All India Conference of Chartered Accountants at Hyderabad (ICAI, Hyderabad, 1993). After the speech, many in the audience who had been strangers before the event acknowledged my presence, as if they knew me, or sought me out for a conversation or a handshake or just to congratulate me. Before my speech, I was a stranger to the audience; after the speech, many people approached me to express their respect and appreciation, which was truly gratifying.

Success as a speaker is based on your ability to connect with the audience. Search for signs of positive affirmation after the speech by connecting with your audience, be it glances, nods, smiles, or eye contact at the coffee table or during the lunch break or in the lift. You may receive remarks directly at the time or later by email like: 'crisp, factual, and impressive'; 'very well appreciated'; 'finest I listened to—very educative experience'; 'active, fruitful participation'. These are the remarks or affirmations indicating that you have connected with the audience, conveyed your message meaningfully, and are on the right track.

## APPLAUSE

Applause during and at the end of your speech is another form of feedback about the success of your speech. Of course, applause at the end will always be there, but the extent and warmth of the applause and the number of times the audience has applauded during the speech are indicators of the extent to which you have connected with the audience. A lukewarm response will indicate the need for improvement and a thunderous applause will boost your confidence.

A standing ovation is the ultimate in appreciation of your speech. During my entire career, I have received a standing ovation only twice. The first time was at my farewell speech on my retirement as a partner from Deloitte (Deloitte, India Partners' Conference, Goa, 2007), and the second occasion was at my farewell speech on retiring as an independent director of Nestlé (Nestlé, Gurugram, 2019). Both were personally touching moments for me.

## CONCLUSION

I am surprised at the number of speakers who are in a rush to catch the next available flight home or to their next destination or who do not even want to stay for the customary after-the-speech tea, lunch, or dinner. Such speakers are denying themselves the valuable gift of feedback which can be truly helpful. Mixing with the crowd after your speech is a great way to pick up signals from them about the impact of your talk.

If you have been a success, many people will cluster around you with a desire to carry on a conversation about the messages conveyed by you in your speech. Invite more people to come and join your small groups of conversationalists. Move from one group of conversationalists to another to solicit as many opinions as you can about your speech. Avoid lingering around any particular group of *fans* for too long.

## FINALLY

Your interaction with the audience is not just restricted to the time that you are on stage for your speech. There is also a prelude and a postscript to your speech that you can use to seek audience reaction. These periods, particularly the postscript, are invaluable for gauging feedback. Please do not deny yourself the opportunity to receive this essential feedback, as it is a must for the self-improvement of your speaking style. *It can reinforce your speaking style and help make you an effective and engaging communicator.*

CHAPTER 52

# COMMUNICATION EVALUATION

*Keep a Standard Checklist Handy*

After your speech is over, dissect it clinically and critically. Get into the habit of debriefing yourself. Recall the audience reaction to the various points that you raised. Do a thorough communication evaluation. Compare your performance against a standard checklist of techniques as described in this book. *Keep a standard checklist handy*. Alternatively, you may make your own personal checklist of techniques that work for you by adding to or subtracting from this standard checklist. Do a personal evaluation by marking or making remarks against each of the following techniques:

## PREPARATION

- audience analysis
- structure
- opening
- closing
- breaks and recaps
- reserve power
- how to practise
- visualization
- visual aids

- stories
- examples and illustrations
- quotations
- variety of multisensory experiences
- memorable moments
- any other item

## PRESENTATION

- speaking style
- possession of your territory
- stance
- choreography
- smile
- eye contact
- voice variation
- downward inflection
- phrase
- pause
- gesture
- body language
- personalization
- humour and wit
- any other item

## RHETORICAL DEVICES

- picture words
- antithesis
- alliteration

- anaphora
- rhetorical question
- metaphor
- hyperbole
- asyndeton
- any other item

## CONCLUSION

- Did you give your audience a variety of multisensory experiences?
- Which particular technique did you use the most?
- Which techniques did you excel in?
- Which techniques require improvement the next time?
- Did you reach out and connect with your audience?
- Were you in total control?
- Summarize your overall efforts in a few sentences.
- Are you prepared to rank yourself?
- Brilliant/Excellent/Good/Average/Poor

CHAPTER 53

# KEEPING A DIARY

*It has Helped me Hugely*

## FAMOUS DIARIES FROM HISTORY: ANNE FRANK AND NELSON MANDELA

In 1942, during World War II, a Jewish teenage girl, forced into hiding in Nazi-occupied Netherlands, started writing a diary. In the diary, she voiced her hopes, vented her frustration, and protested the injustice around her. Her diary inspired millions around the world. Many films, documentaries, and television serials have been made on her short life. Her name was Anne Frank.

Nelson Mandela's moving and compelling diary was published as a book titled *Conservations with Myself.* It shows the inner workings of one of the most inspiring leaders in history. The diary records Mandela's intimate thoughts and ideas throughout his life, from his travails under imprisonment to becoming the leader of a free country.

## MY DIARY

I am no Anne Frank or Nelson Mandela. However, I too kept a diary of my speeches. If you are going to be a long-term player in the arena of public speaking and genuinely want to excel, then you should keep a diary in which you enter comments and self-analyses after each speaking occasion. The only reason that I have been able to give particulars of my speeches is because of the entries in my diary. These elements are recorded in my diary which otherwise would have faded from my memory with the passage of time.

I am giving you a peep into my diary by reproducing below the notes taken in respect of four speeches. These notes appear as they were entered, except for some minor editing and formatting. These notes touch upon what was done well and what needed to be improved. I recommend that if you are serious about improving your speaking skills, you should start keeping notes in a diary after every speech. *It has helped me hugely*. It will help you too.

## PERSONAL EXAMPLES

1. 13th All India Conference of Chartered Accountants, Hyderabad, 1993

   Did well:

   - authority
   - alliteration, antithesis, anaphora, and repetition
   - pause
   - golden words
   - empathy with audience by using local examples
   - personalization

   To improve:

   - eye contact
   - humour
   - change of tone
   - dialogue
   - breaks and recaps

2. National Electricity Authority Workshop, Kathmandu, Nepal, 1994

   Did well:

   - visual as an introduction for the first time
   - personal anecdotes
   - eye contact
   - possession of my territory
   - personalization
   - closing visual
   - humour
   - anaphora, antithesis, repetition, and asyndeton

   To improve:

   - resonance
   - pause
   - downward inflection
   - change of tone

3. Association of U.K. Chartered Accountants, New Delhi, 1994

   Did well:

   - specifics
   - quotations
   - structure
   - opening
   - personalization
   - audience empathy
   - possession of my territory

   To improve:

   - eye contact

- pause
- change of tone

4. Australian Business Delegation, Federation of Indian Chambers of Commerce and Industry, New Delhi, 1996

   Did well:

   - phrase
   - change of tone
   - authority
   - downward inflexion
   - pause
   - structure
   - style
   - specifics
   - body language

   To improve:

   - develop usage of more picture words
   - develop during daily conversation more of pause and downward inflection
   - develop more eye contact; look at some members of audience for longer

## CONCLUSION

Evaluate your oratorical skills by jotting down notes in a diary after the event. Such observations help you to record your own personal assessment of how well you delivered your speech according to certain set parameters and identify the areas where you need to improve. This can be a great self-tool in improving your speaking skills. Analyse your weaknesses and work hard to overcome them. Analyse your strengths and incorporate them in the next speech you give because you know these tactics have worked well and have proven their worth.

CHAPTER 54

# EXAMPLE OF VARIETY IN A SPEECH

*This Wonderful Self-Analytical Tool Yields useful Results*

## PERSONAL EXAMPLE

I was requested by Suresh Subramanian, Partner, S. R. Batliboi Associates, member firm of EY, India to deliver a speech of sixty minutes on 'Frauds in India' to a select audience of about fifty managers and partners at Chennai (EY, India, 2020). I was delighted to accept, as frauds is one of my favourite topics. From my final speaking notes and prompt cards, I did a self-analysis of the various speaking techniques used by me for this speech.

I counted the following number of times I used the techniques listed below in my speech on frauds in order to create variety and give the audience a multisensory experience. There is no standard number of times for each constituent, but I do try to include as many different categories as possible. From the listing below, what clearly stands out is my preference for *examples and illustrations*—which I used eleven times.

## FINDINGS

In my speech on frauds, the list of speaking techniques used and the number of times that each technique was used, as given in brackets, are indicated below:

- examples and illustrations (11)
- alliteration (4)
- metaphor (3)

- contrast (2)
- personalization (2)
- rhetorical question (2)
- anaphora (2)
- asyndeton (1)
- analogy (1)
- pause (1)

## WONDERFUL SELF-ANALYTICAL TOOL

This is a *wonderful self-analytical tool* to apply to some of your speeches from your final notes, as it can give you a clue about your particular preferences and speaking style. It will bring into sharp focus your modus operandi or game plan. It is not necessary that for each speech the numbers should be the same. This self-analysis will help you identify the absence of any particular method that you should be adding to your repertoire of speaking strategies. For example, from such an analysis you may find that you seldom include humour or alliteration in your speech. This will alert you to your own shortcomings and help you design a better speech next time. Sprinkling a dose of different recipes creates variety in your speaking style and makes for listener awareness. Those who want to improve their speaking style should do this exercise in self-reflection.

## FINALLY

The really complete speaker deals with both style and content and stands out in both areas. The natural speaker is in total control of the speaking situation, from planning through to delivery. To be able to do this on a regular basis, learn the art of honest reflection after each speech.

CHAPTER 55

# MY MOST DIFFICULT AUDIENCE ANALYSIS

*Become Audience Centric and not Speaker Centric*

One of the biggest errors that speakers make is that they concentrate totally on the substance of their speech, and forget about conducting audience analysis. I am not saying content is not relevant—of course, it is relevant—but first comes audience analysis. A better understanding of the nature of the audience helps tremendously in focusing on the composition of your speech.

## PERSONAL EXAMPLE

I was once requested to give a presentation to a group of visiting French accountants on 'Indian accounting standards' organized by the French Embassy (French Embassy, New Delhi, 1996). My audience analysis showed the following salient features:

- My audience were French accountants visiting India along with their spouses.
- My audience were on a holiday in India and not on a business trip.
- My audience, including the spouses, would be arriving at the conference hall immediately after shopping.
- My audience did not fully understand English.

- An interpreter would translate my speech as I was speaking.
- The event was being organized by the French Embassy.

Clearly, my audience analysis gave me important clues as to how to compose my presentation:

- Should not be too technical, as spouses would also be present.
- Should be light-hearted as this was not a business delegation, but a holiday trip.
- Should use humour as the audience were coming to the conference hall straight from shopping.
- Should use body language more as the audience did not fully understand English.
- Should have numerous French examples and references.

If I had merely concentrated in showing off my knowledge of 'Indian accounting standards' with data, facts, and statistics—as I was greatly tempted to do—I would have failed in connecting with my French audience and also failed as a speaker. If I had focused on giving the standard speech on accounting standards as typically given to an audience of young accounting students in training, or to seasoned audit managers, I would have missed the bus by a mile, besides being monotonous and boring.

## BUILDING EMPATHY AND HARMONY

Instead, as part of my research for the speech, I made a list of all the French companies operating in India, like BNP Paribas, Schneider Electric, and Peugeot. I included in the speech numerous French examples and references, to the French language, French GDP, and French infrastructure. I endeared myself to the audience because I gave a lot of French examples, articulated well, showed enthusiasm, adopted a good stance, used quotations, and employed powerful openings and closings. My speaking style appeared extemporaneous and relaxed, backed by prompt cards and some supporting slides.

Clarity was crucial, so it was necessary to pay extra attention to structure and recaps in my speech. Again, gestures and body language, analogies and comparisons, assumed more prominence. I was flexible in my approach and deleted the more technical parts of my speech because of the presence of spouses, the casual dress of the audience, and the generally carefree holiday mood.

I opted for a judicious mix of my usual material on accounting standards with plenty of soft breaks to lighten the moment. As this was a light-hearted occasion and by no means a business presentation, I introduced humour, wit, asides, and repartee at various places in my speech. I used humour and wit much more than I would normally do in a speech. This turned out to be a big crowd-pleaser as it was appropriate, spontaneous, and was in harmony with the atmosphere and mood of the audience.

The success of a speech is gauged by the response from the audience and by their repeated applause, and not how well you think you have prepared your material. Content is relevant, but delivery is essential. If your delivery is off target because of poor audience analysis, then even the most brilliant material will fall flat.

## LESSONS FOR ME

Though this was an exceptional case, nevertheless it highlighted some critical lessons for me. This was an unusual case of a serious topic like Indian accounting standards under discussion, addressed to an audience of French accountants, with their spouses, who were on holiday in India. Their attendance at the conference in casual attire after a bout of shopping further highlighted the lightness of the moment. This particular experience taught me how crucial it was to first spend time and effort in analysing the audience carefully, as also the occasion, before developing the substance of any speech.

## FINALLY

Follow this fundamental rule: first comes analysis of the audience; subsequently comes the content of the speech. *Become audience centric and not speaker centric.*

CHAPTER 56

# MY MOST DIFFICULT SPEAKING ASSIGNMENT

*A Good Story Wins Every Time over Overwhelming Facts and Figures*

## DEALING WITH NUMEROUS UNKNOWNS

In 1993, I was requested by the senior partner of my firm, A. F. Ferguson & Co., to join the delegation led by the Federation of Indian Chambers of Commerce and Industry (FICCI) to the United States to promote foreign investment in India, pursuant to India's liberalization beginning in 1991 (FICCI, United States, 1993). I was given the task of speaking on 'Taxation in India'. The talks were to be held at six cities, namely Washington, D.C., New York, Chicago, Miami, San Jose, and Los Angeles.

This was my most difficult speaking assignment ever. This was a huge challenge to me as I was still cutting my teeth in the art of public speaking, but was also a great opportunity to put into actual practice some of the methodologies relating to public speaking that I was then studying and seeking to master. I was relatively young in speech craft and was still developing an overall game plan or modus operandi for all my speeches. My analysis of the speaking situation in the United States indicated:

- unknown audience
- unknown co-speakers
- unknown sponsors
- unknown locations

This was totally different from the speaking situations that I had faced in India. In India, very often, the audiences were known to me, together with the sponsors and co-speakers and even sometimes the locations. I was now about to speak in a foreign country, which I had never visited before, at six different locations, before unknown audiences and with sponsors and co-speakers whom I did not know.

One thing was clear—my preparation for the speeches involving the gathering of extra material and the building of reserve power would have to be very extensive. My visualization of the speaking events in the six cities would have to be very thorough. I needed to recall all my past successful speeches through visualization as a confidence booster. I would have to make a special effort to visit the conference halls at each of the hotels where we would be staying so I could familiarize myself with the speaking locations. I would have to practise the delivery of my material far more meticulously than I usually did. I started reading books on public speaking extensively.

This was a trip to promote American investment in India, with very little time for acclimatization to the city or for getting to know my co-speakers. As the trip progressed from city to city, familiarity with the rest of the delegates developed, and with familiarity came confidence. By the time we arrived at the last city on our tour, Los Angeles, I was speaking like a veteran and the feedback that I was receiving on my speeches was very encouraging.

## FEEDBACK

This was the first time that I extensively used the technique of including in my speeches more examples, illustrations, and case studies, and fewer facts and figures and less data. I found that this strategy produced astounding results. I realized that not only was I connecting quite well with my unknown audiences, unknown co-speakers, and unknown sponsors, but also, most importantly, they were remembering the examples I was citing in my speeches.

Two years later, I met Dr Amit Mitra, the chairman of my sessions in the United States, who subsequently became secretary general, FICCI, and thereafter the finance minister of West Bengal. He still remembered the example of Modi Xerox that I had given in my speeches in the United States to explain the liberalization of foreign investment in India from the tax and legal angles, notwithstanding the fact that two years had elapsed. Two members from the audience at San Jose, M. Laetsch and John Laetsch, met me at a private dinner in New Delhi two months later and remembered my presentation as being full of 'vigor and vim'. An industrialist who was part of the delegation, N.R. Narayana Murthy, one of the founders of Infosys, on his return to India wrote to me saying, 'Your presentation was perhaps the finest I listened to at Washington, New York, and San Jose. It was a very educative experience for me.'

## GIVE THE AUDIENCE A LAYER CAKE OF EXAMPLES AND STORIES

There was no doubt in my mind that the cutting down on the amount of information that I was giving in my speeches in the form of facts, figures, and statistics was the primary reason that my speeches became more memorable and impactful. Too many people believe that the way to deliver a speech is to inundate the audience with lots of facts and figures combined with lots of charts, graphs, and slides. They are wrong. If I had followed the numbers-driven approach, because I believed that I had a great deal to tell and had wanted to show off my knowledge of Indian tax laws, my speech would have been monotonous and tedious, and hence a flop.

## FINALLY

For my six speeches in the United States, I considered another approach—to tell the audiences a story—specifically, the Modi Xerox story. I realized that *a good story wins every time over overwhelming facts and figures.* Since 1993, I have stuck to this blueprint or game plan as a winning formula by giving the audience a layer cake of relevant examples, appropriate illustrations, and engaging stories.

CHAPTER 57

# EXAMPLE OF A WRITTEN MEMORIAL SPEECH

*Use Alliteration, Antithesis, and Anaphora for Impact*

## OFFICIAL WRITTEN MEMORIAL SPEECH

I seldom write and read a speech. Most of my presentations have been executed through what appears to be an extempore speech, albeit supported by prompt cards, but is backed by hours of solid practice and preparation. The exception was the memorial speech for S.P. Godrej, Chairman Emeritus, WWF-India, which I delivered by reading in my official position as Vice-President, WWF-India on 12 June 2000 in the WWF-India auditorium (WWF-India, New Delhi, 2000).

Readers will recognize the use of picture words, alliteration, antithesis, anaphora, and repetition in the written speech.

Here is the entire speech as written and delivered.

## EULOGY

Seven years ago, I met Sohrab Godrej for the first time at my first trustee meeting of WWF-India of which he was the founder trustee. We met here in the boardroom in this very building where today we are all assembled to pay homage and to grace his memory.

During these seven years that I knew Sohrab Godrej, I came to realize very fast and quickly that he was a man of many causes, and there were two in particular which were very paramount and dear to his heart. Population and tigers. He lamented the fact that India was fast hurtling to a population of one billion people—over three times the population at the time of our independence, and he was anguished at the steady decimation of the majestic animal, the tiger, which he feared may soon become extinguished.

But the man was more than the causes he stood for and fought for so gallantly. He had the unique ability of being able to reach out and connect with people. When we first met seven years ago, there was nothing really in common between us—we had no common ground. This simple but extraordinary man was already an established crusader for the environment. I was a hard-nosed finance man. He knew very little of finance. I knew even less of the environment. He lived permanently in the city of Mumbai. I lived here in Delhi. Yet Sohrab Godrej was able to break through these barriers so fast that soon he was contacting me all the time, where ever I was. Sometimes at Delhi or Mumbai or Pune or even Goa.

In addition to Sohrab Godrej's remarkable ability to connect with people in a very humane and enduring way, there was another side to his personality which I was soon to learn and admire—his ability to be compassionate. During the last seven years, we must have had over thirty trustee meetings of WWF-India, and, believe me, some of them were very stormy meetings—very often over Project Tiger or funding for the tiger or some other special issue. If there was one trustee, amongst all trustees, who could look at the storm brewing in the boardroom with a steady eye, who could be cool, composed, and compassionate to all points of view, it was Sohrab Godrej. He could think ill of no one, not even one whose views were totally different to his.

A few days before he left in mid-May on what was to be his last journey, a hectic journey as was his style, he contacted me and we spoke for about ten minutes. He spoke about the concerns about the funding for the tiger project, particularly under the new arrangements. He touched upon the past, the past seven years, and some of the issues that we had faced together. It appears to me now that he was doing a historical recount, a kind of review, as if he had a premonition that soon he was to be no more. And when on the morning of Monday, May 23rd' I read in the newspapers that he indeed was no more, I felt saddened that all of us, particularly the WWF-India family, would never again see this door, on the left-hand side, open and Sohrab Godrej walk in as he had done on so many numerous occasions in the past, with his impish smile and half-chuckle.

Sohrab Godrej is no more, but he leaves behind a legion of friends and admirers. He leaves behind a rich and enduring legacy; a legacy of friendship; a legacy of compassion; a legacy of a passionate commitment to social causes to which he contributed with rich and ready endowments.

I would like to conclude my memorial on behalf of the entire WWF family in India and International, on behalf of its staff, founder trustees, past and current trustees, to Sohrab Godrej, founder trustee, past president, chairman emeritus of WWF-India, with a fond farewell in these words: Here was a man who had much, but who gave to others much more. Here was a man who had malice towards none, with charity for all. May his soul rest in eternal peace.

## FINALLY

It was an honour to have been asked to deliver this eulogy for S.P. Godrej, a man whose life work I had much admired and who was a doyen in the world of conservation.

# Part Five

# REGULATORY BODIES AND LAW COURTS

CHAPTER 58

# HOW TO FACE REGULATORY BODIES AND LAW COURTS

Establish Proper Eye Contact

## PERSONAL EXAMPLE

In 1985, at the time of the Tri-Sure India Ltd fraud case, things were simpler and there was not a multiplicity of regulators. As the principal in charge of the audit, I was one of the main witnesses to be examined on behalf of the defendants, A.F. Ferguson & Co., in the fraud case before the Bombay High Court. I faced a hostile and confrontational learned counsel for the plaintiffs and his team. I underwent dogged and determined cross-examination in the witness box. I was alluded to as a failed chartered accountant who had qualified in the United Kingdom and who was not familiar with auditing practices in India. The experience left me shattered.

1. *Damage to professional reputation.* I realized that an unfavourable decision would cause immediate and far-reaching damage to my professional reputation. An adverse order could cause serious injury to my professional reputation, an injury not capable of being entirely repaired or healed subsequently. To many people, their professional reputation is their most valued and cherished possession. At the age of forty-three, I was still relatively young in my profession and was scrupulously, conscientiously, and diligently building my career as well as my professional honour and reputation.

2. *Found not guilty.* You can imagine my palpable relief when, ultimately, the firm was held not guilty of the charges levied against it. The Honourable Justice M.L. Pendse held: 'The evidence led by the plaintiffs in the present case falls far short of the requisite proof to prove that the auditors were guilty of negligence in the discharge of their duties.'
3. *Eye contact.* I had limited knowledge and no experience of how to speak in a public forum. I was untutored, except to the extent that I had been told by my defending learned counsel to look the presiding honourable judge in the eye (eye contact) and not to lean against the wooden rails of the witness box in desperation (balanced stance). For some strategic reason, I was also advised to keep a watch on the courtroom clock, particularly just before the recess. The rest is history.
4. *Rule of primacy and recency.* Much later I realized that the learned counsel for the plaintiffs was following the rule of primacy and recency; it is also called the serial position effect. This is an influential technique used by trial lawyers to make the openings and closings of their arguments powerful and memorable. The rule of primacy says to lead off with your strongest statement. The rule of recency says to finish with your most powerful punch. Usually, this is a matter of using your strongest point in one place and your next strongest point in the other. This theory or law is based on the tendency of listeners to remember beginnings and endings.

## HOW DOES THE AUDITOR DEFEND HIMSELF?

I have had my fair share of facing fraud situations and of dealing with regulators during my career in India—including the Registrar of Companies, special investigators, the disciplinary committee of the Institute of Chartered Accountants of India, and the Bombay High Court.

How does the auditor defend himself against allegations or charges before regulatory bodies or in law courts? I appreciate that at times the defendant auditor is represented by a team of lawyers and counsels who argue the case. However, in many instances, the auditor has to make representations. In such a scenario, a strategy based on the following techniques will be handy.

- Be in total command of the subject matter under scrutiny.
- Quiet the mind before the interrogation.
- Practise being in the eye of the storm.
- Do yoga and meditation.
- Do pranayama.
- Do relaxation exercises.
- Calm yourself through visualization.
- Establish proper eye contact.
- Adopt a proper balanced stance.
- Smile often and do not frown.
- Use gestures.
- Use confident body language.
- Introduce humour and wit.
- Use picture words.
- Use similes and metaphors.
- Discard arrogance, belligerence, and sarcasm.
- Subjugate the ego.
- Display honesty, decency, sincerity, passion, and humility.
- Keep your tranquility and composure.
- Emulate the traits of stillness and calmness of the praying mantis.

- Never be in a hurry to finish, but keep a discreet eye on the clock.
- Be aware of the doctrine of primacy and recency.
- Try to gain and maintain professional detachment.
- Tread softly to go far.

Many of these methods are aimed at improving speaking skills, as discussed in various chapters in this book. Without diminishing the other techniques, I would rank establishing *proper eye contact* as essential. In addition, you need to quiet the mind, keep your tranquility and composure, acquire professional detachment, and subjugate the ego.

## LINCOLN AND CHURCHILL

In his book *Abraham Lincoln and the Second American Revolution,* James M. McPherson has a chapter called 'How Lincoln Won the War with Metaphors' in which he examines Lincoln's skilful use of words, and his soaring oratory, to inspire people during the Civil War (1861–1865) in the United States to fight for victory.

In another historic instance, Kennedy praised Churchill's speechwriting achievements, and particularly his ability to move and inspire his countrymen during very turbulent and trying times: 'In the dark days and darker nights when England stood alone—and most men, save Englishmen, despaired of England's life—he mobilized the English language and sent it into battle. The incandescent quality of his words illuminated the courage of his countrymen.'

These lessons from history about the impact of great leaders and statesmen, especially during difficult times, are worthy of study. We can take inspiration from their powerful and inspiring words to guide our own actions when we face tough situations.

## FINALLY

It is the task of the regulator to validate the case as much as it is the job of the defendant to rebut the allegations. You may not be a Lincoln or a Churchill. Nevertheless, the ability to communicate clearly and persuasively, skilfully and competently, before regulatory bodies and in law courts makes a big difference. Accomplished defendants with good communication skills have a considerable edge over those who don't have these skills, and hence have a *better chance of winning the war.*

# Part Six

# CONCLUSION

CHAPTER 59

# YOGA

*Practise Pranayama, Yogic Breathing Exercises*

I have been doing yoga and public speaking for many years and for me, the two are intimately linked. Breathing and relaxation play a significant role in public speaking as in yoga. Yoga, the ancient art of relaxation and meditation, has helped me to remain cool and collected by removing any stress arising from a speaking situation. Yoga is derived from a Sanskrit word meaning 'to join' or 'to unite'. The union refers to the joining of our mind with our body.

Today, our exposure to yoga is largely restricted to over 300 physical postures or asanas. Hence, it is important to narrow down a few easy poses to start our daily yoga routine. Yoga is non-competitive in nature. You practise and progress at your own pace and schedule.

Yoga's benefits are both physical and mental. It increases flexibility and fitness, relieves muscle tension, enhances core strength, reduces mental stress, and promotes calmness and serenity.

## YOGA AND STRETCHES

Yoga involves a series of stretches along with other exercises. The stretches focus on specific areas, usually those that tend to become constricted, like the neck, shoulders, back, hips, legs, and spine. These exercises can be extended to the lips, tongue, and cheeks. Some stretches are done standing, some lying on the back, and some lying on the stomach. Yoga can be built into one's schedule as and when convenient. There is no fixed prescription regarding timing and duration. You can do yoga for five minutes, thirty minutes, or forty-five minutes, or even more. The effects are amazing. After just a few minutes, you feel more open, relaxed, and energized.

## YOGA AND BREATHING

In yoga, the focus is on deep, smooth, and controlled inhalation and exhalation that initiates each movement of the body. Paying attention to one's breathing is helpful in managing nervousness associated with public speaking. When speakers get anxious, their breathing tends to be rapid and shallow, causing them to speak fast. Consciously deepening and slowing the breath, especially right before you speak when nervousness generally spikes, can help lower the heart rate and allow for a louder, richer, and slower vocal quality.

Nothing is faster or more reliable for reducing acute mental and emotional distress than calm, controlled, diaphragmatic breathing. In yoga, this is called *pranayama,* a Sanskrit word that means *breath control.*

## YOGA AND PUBLIC SPEAKING

Yoga and public speaking both involve focused and regulated breathing. In yoga, you seek to link your breath with each movement or asana, which results in attentive, controlled breathing. In public speaking, you focus on deep, slow breathing, which enables you to speak with resonance, cadence, and modulation, and allows you to overcome stage fright and nervousness. Hence, proper breathing is very important.

Breathing is as fundamental to relaxation as it is to life itself. Because proper, self-aware breathing helps you achieve a state of ease and relaxation, this technique can relieve the tension of a speaking situation. It reduces nervousness by releasing the excess energy you hold inside in the form of tension. It increases your ability to speak at length without tiring or gasping.

## SPEAK FROM THE GUT

Speak from the gut is a popular instruction in public speaking. Ground your voice deep in your chest or diaphragm. Oxygen is the source of power for speech, so make sure you allow it to sink deep down into your body. When you inhale and exhale, your abdomen moves in and out. When you breathe deeply, right down into your diaphragm, you are also helping to ground yourself. When sound emanates from your gut, it will have depth and resonance. This will contribute to a strong and impressive voice, one that can fill a room and mark your presence.

## FINALLY

Doing yoga regularly can enhance your public speaking skills. It can help control stage fright and overcome nervousness. It can help in projecting a resonant and well-modulated voice with proper pacing and cadence.

CHAPTER 60

# SPEECH IMPEDIMENT

*A Speech Impediment is not a Barrier to Success in Public Speaking*

## CHURCHILL

Churchill who is acclaimed as one of the greatest orators of the twentieth century had a slight speech impediment. There seems to be some controversy as to whether or not he had a lisp, a stutter, or both. Churchill definitely was self-conscious about his elocution and diligently practised speaking clearly, rehearsing his speeches and avoiding, whenever possible, words that began or ended with an 's'. He overcame the problem to become a stirring and eloquent speaker, giving us some of the most memorable words in history. Churchill's speeches may appear to be extemporaneous, but they were backed by hours and hours of solid drills.

## KING GEORGE VI

King George VI, who was painfully shy and had stuttered since childhood, loathed public speaking because of his speech impediment. He eventually overcame his stammer and conquered his anxiety and dread with the help of an Australian speech therapist, Lionel Logue. Thanks to Logue's somewhat unconventional techniques, George VI gained self-confidence and his public speaking improved. His relationship with Logue is captured in the Oscar-winning 2010 movie *The King's Speech*. George VI's inspiring live radio address on 3 September 1939, announcing that Britain would be going to war against Germany, is evidence of his determination and will to triumph over his affliction. He became a symbol of hope and strength for the British people during the dark days of World War II and beyond, restoring their faith in the country's monarchy.

## PALKHIVALA

In my younger days, I often listened to the speeches of the well-known Indian jurist and lawyer Nani Palkhivala, particularly his brilliant summaries of the annual budgets, which appeared extemporaneous, but were in reality the result of many hours of hard practice. For many Indians, what Palkhivala had to say after the presentation of the budget was perhaps more important than the finance minister's speech in Parliament. But it might astonish many to learn that this eloquent and polished speaker had a stammer when he was young and had shied away from speaking in public, just like Churchill, who also had a speech impediment.

## BIDEN

Joseph R. Biden, Jr. has overcome a severe and lifelong stutter and gone on to became a lawyer, senator, vice president, and now president of the United States. As a political leader and statesman, Biden is frequently required to speak in public at high-profile events. Despite his speech impediment, he has forged a highly successful political career and has sound advice for others who struggle with a stutter. In 2015, Biden wrote a letter to the Stuttering Foundation of America: 'If I could share one piece of advice with all of those struggling with a stutter, it would be this: When you commit yourself to a goal and when you persevere in the face of struggle, you will discover new strengths and skills to help you overcome not only this challenge, but future life challenges as well. I promise you—you have nothing to be ashamed of, and you have every reason to be proud.'

## FINALLY

All of them—Churchill, George VI, Palkhivala, Biden—overcame their speech handicaps through hard work, diligence, and practice and made a mark in their chosen fields. *A speech impediment is not a barrier to success in public speaking*, nor a hurdle in a career that involves a lot of speaking, like those of a politician, leader, lawyer, or actor.

CHAPTER 61

# STAGE FRIGHT

*Begin Small, then Go Big*
*Begin with the Known, Then Go to the Unknown*

Every speaker is prone to stage fright to some degree. I have found that I can reduce my stage fright and nervousness by paying close attention to the topics discussed in the chapters listed below. If you read or reread these chapters, you will know how to handle and minimize stage fright.

## SPEAKING STRATEGY

Every speaker, especially those who deliver presentations often, should develop a speaking strategy. Build bit by bit, starting with known audiences and familiar topics, and then move to unknown audiences and more challenging subjects. First, engage in speaking performances in a known environment to gain confidence before taking up unfamiliar topics. In the early part of my speaking career, I took small steps. I participated regularly in conferences organized by a leading client, DCM Ltd, speaking on topics that I was familiar with. This was where I cut my teeth in the art of public speaking. It was a wonderful learning experience; I spoke before small groups of accountants, all known to me, in a convivial atmosphere. Start with small audiences of twenty or thirty before graduating to audiences of 800 or 1,000. How can you get stage fright if you begin like I did—in a small way?

## STRUCTURE (CHAPTER 2)

If you have developed a proper structure for your speech, with an orderly progression of ideas, it will prevent you from getting derailed.

## BREAKS AND RECAPS (CHAPTER 4)

If you have mastered the technique of transitions, through adequate breaks and recaps, it will provide a cushion and help reduce stage fright.

## GATHERING THE MATERIAL (CHAPTER 5)

Be meticulous and patient in gathering and understanding your material. The better you grasp what you are talking about, and the more deeply you care about the topic, the less likely you are to make a mistake or go off track. And if you do get lost, you will be able to recover quickly.

## RESERVE POWER (CHAPTER 7)

If you assemble many more thoughts, or points of discussion, than you are likely to need, you will never be at a loss for words. Keep your speech short and focused, and keep plenty of ammunition (in your speaker's arsenal) in case you need to use it.

## PRACTICE (CHAPTER 9)

Practise your complete presentation several times. Practise, practise, practise your speech so that it appears extempore. The purpose is not to memorize what you are going to say, but rather to become thoroughly familiar with the key points and insights as well as the flow of ideas. I put in a lot of relentless practice. For me, a minimum of twelve training sessions from the time that my final prompt cards are ready are a prerequisite. If you invest this kind of time and effort in your preparation, you will never really feel stage fright.

## EXERCISES (CHAPTER 11)

Breathing exercises, physical exercises, and power stretches on D-Day can all be very calming and helpful in fighting anxiety. Do some physical exercise in the morning before your speech, like playing badminton or going for a run, and see how this lessens anxiety. Just before you get up to the podium, and during your speech, take two or more deep and slow breaths.

## VISUALIZATION (CHAPTER 12)

Imagine that your presentation will go well. Positive thoughts can help decrease negativity about your performance and relieve anxiety to some degree. Overcoming your anxiety step by step through visualization is an essential tool for delivering successful speeches. Engage in desensitization procedures and imagine yourself performing successfully. Do this a number of times till you gain confidence. Consequently, you will build up expectation of mastery at the actual performance. Visualization helps in combatting stage fright.

## QUIETING THE MIND (CHAPTER 20)

To quiet the mind and gain confidence on the day of the speaking event, do yoga and meditation, perform stretching exercises, go for a run, listen to classical music, dress well. All this will help you counter stage fright.

## YOGA (CHAPTER 59)

Paying attention to breathing is helpful in managing nervousness associated with public speaking. Perform pranayama, yogic breathing exercises, regularly.

## FINALLY

The more speeches you give, the sooner you will get over stage fright. It is a matter of gaining confidence one speech at a time. It is a matter of routine, repetition, rehearsal, and constant practice. Soon you will discover, as many speakers have done, that by getting successful speaking experiences behind you, public speaking will become a joy and a pleasure. *Begin small, then go big. Begin with the known, then go to the unknown.*

CHAPTER 62

# LINCOLN, CHURCHILL, AND HITLER

*Carve out your Own Speaking Style*

## LINCOLN

Lincoln came from a poor rural background and worked on a dirt farm. He was a self-taught man who lived close to the rhythms of nature. In his younger days, Lincoln often made a round trip of thirty to forty miles on foot to hear famous speakers. He would come home so stirred, so determined to be a speaker that he would gather the other hired workers about him in the fields and, mounting a stump, make speeches and tell them stories. He rehearsed his speeches everywhere—in the fields, in the woods, before crowds. He joined literary and debating societies and practised speaking on the topics of the day.

He honed his storytelling skills until he eventually became a master storyteller. A study of Lincoln's speeches reveals that he frequently used images and figurative language, of which metaphor was the most common. His speeches and letters abound with metaphors, particularly animal-related metaphors, which had the persuasive power of concreteness and clarity.

Eventually, Lincoln became the president of the United States and immediately faced the secession of the southern states from the Union over the issue of slavery and states' rights, resulting in the American Civil War. Some historians argue that Lincoln won the Civil War because he was able to communicate in a clear and forceful manner, whereas his opponent, Jefferson Davis, the president of the Confederate States of America, thought more in abstractions and spoke in platitudes, delivering speeches that were stiff, cold, and logical. Lincoln was by far the more inspiring leader who energized and mobilized his people to make the sacrifices necessary for victory.

## CHURCHILL

Churchill was not born a master orator. He overcame a childhood lisp by practising enunciation. He understood the power of words early in his career. After a disastrous experience trying to address the House of Commons entirely from memory, he abandoned the practice of giving memorized speeches. Instead, he spent hours preparing a single speech, sometimes to the accompaniment of martial music being played on gramophone records, working at it repeatedly until he had it just right.

Churchill employed short words, memorable phrases, and evocative images, and his extraordinary speeches hinged on a series of classical rhetorical devices. His speeches were full of rhetoric, with generous use of alliteration, anaphora, antithesis, and asyndeton. Churchill is best remembered as the British prime minister whose speeches rallied a nation facing a relentless onslaught by Nazi Germany during the Second World War.

In his first speech as prime minister to the House of Commons on 13 May 1940, Churchill used the memorable phrase which over time has been enshrined in the history books: 'I have nothing to offer but blood, toil, tears and sweat.' At the height of the Second World War, and during their darkest hour, Churchill's dramatic and powerful speeches served to shore up the spirits and strengthen the resolve of the British people.

## HITLER

Hitler understood early on that leaders have to be actors. As a young man, he studied the performances of a Bavarian comedian in order to learn how to captivate an audience. He examined the comedian's timing, delivery, and techniques and diligently rehearsed his own poses, gestures, and facial expressions in front of a mirror. He made speeches before small audiences in the streets and beer halls of Munich to hone his public speaking skills. There he learnt the significance of careful planning and thorough preparation of material. He learnt how to change his tone and vary his pitch to rouse his audience.

Hitler worked hard at his delivery, hand gestures, and body language since these non-verbal elements constituted half his message. His personal photographer took several photos of Hitler's facial expressions and gestures while he rehearsed his upcoming speeches in front of a mirror. After studying the photos, Hitler asked for them to be destroyed as he wanted no record of this to survive. However, the photographer saved the photographs and published them in his memoirs many years later. Hitler became Chancellor of Germany in 1933 and eventually started the Second World War with the invasion of Poland in 1939.

## CONCLUSION

Lincoln, Churchill, and Hitler were not born speakers; they acquired their oratorical skills by following a hard drill. All three have gone down in history as highly effective and brilliant speakers, but they learnt the art and trained themselves: Lincoln, by walking miles through fields to listen to skilled orators of his times and becoming a master storyteller; Churchill, through hours of practising, with martial music playing in the background, and relying on short words and rhetorical devices; and Hitler, through the careful study of the performances of comedians and by diligently practising his gestures and body language. Each perfected his own particular style and manner and achieved remarkable success as public speakers: Lincoln, by storytelling; Churchill, by using short words and rhetoric; and Hitler, by employing distinctive hand gestures and body language.

## FINALLY

An examination of the divergent speaking styles of these three formidable political figures from history is a tremendous learning for potential public speakers. The most important takeaways are: be comfortable with your own individual style and manner, let your true personality shine, and follow your own chosen track. Do not attempt to be a Lincoln or Churchill or Hitler. Do not mimic or copy others. *Carve out your own speaking style* and be true to yourself.

# CHAPTER 63

# PUBLIC SPEAKING FOR STUDENTS

*Read this Book and Go for It*

## PERSONALLY

I regret that I started my journey of public speaking in a serious manner on the back of the Tri-Sure India Ltd fraud case when I was already in my forties. It took the impact of this case to jolt me into learning the art of public speaking. In hindsight, I regret that as a student I did not participate in debates or plays in school and college, which would have helped me build a wider vocabulary, equipped me with the fundamentals of elocution and proper articulation, and instilled confidence in me from a young age.

I further regret that as a student at Oxford University, I missed out on learning the skill of public speaking by not becoming a member of the famous Oxford Union, the largest and most celebrated debating society in the world, a unique institution where some of the world's most powerful and impressive figures share their most personal stories. Such opportunities come rarely.

My advice to students is to grab every opportunity that comes their way and give priority to the acquisition of competence in public speaking. This skill will stand them in good stead later in life.

## ENGAGE IN SPEAKING ACTIVITIES

India today has a unique opportunity to harness the potential and energy of a large young population. This 'demographic dividend' is expected to last for the next twenty years at least. While the availability of employment will always be contingent on a growing economy, the better jobs, entrepreneurial opportunities, and leadership positions are likely to go to those who have good skills in speaking and presentation. So it makes sense for students to build their skills and abilities from a young age.

Students can hone their speaking and presentation skills in many ways, in both formal and informal settings. Formal settings include making class presentations, participating in debates and discussions, and addressing the school assembly. More relaxed settings include extracurricular activities like dramatics, webcasts, quiz programmes, and just about any opportunity that gets students in front of an audience.

## PARTICIPATE IN QUIZ PROGRAMMES

Participating in quiz programmes is an excellent way for students to acclimatize to a public forum. Quizzing is both fun and educational. It allows students to perform on a public platform in a non-threatening environment.

Let me give you two examples. *Saevus Magazine*, one of India's foremost nature and wildlife magazines, in association with Rotary Clubs and schools across the country, organizes quiz programmes championing the cause of the natural world. WWF-India, a leading conservation organization, runs an annual Wild Wisdom Quiz for schools. The objective of the quiz is to raise awareness about India's flora and fauna and to inculcate a sense of pride amongst students in India's rich natural heritage.

## A MATTER OF CHOICE AND NOT FORCE

Public speaking can be unnerving for even experienced speakers, so it is understandable that school students who are still developing their speaking skills may feel particularly apprehensive. Luckily, they can learn to deal with their fears with the help of technology. Students can use numerous public speaking apps to overcome their fear of public speaking.

However, as speaking in public may cause anxiety, students should not be forced to do something that makes them uncomfortable. Even though speaking in front of the class is supposed to build one's confidence and may even be a part of schoolwork, I think if it leads to students feeling unsettled and anxious, the school authorities should probably provide an exit route for such students. Forcing timid and diffident students to make presentations in front of their peers can cause additional stress and problems.

In view of this, training in public speaking at a young age should not be compulsory. Only those who are interested and willing, and have the aptitude to undergo intensive self-training on a voluntary basis, should proceed. It should be a matter of choice and not force.

## LEARN FROM YOUR MISTAKES

If you make a mistake, let it go. Do not brood over it too much. Do not get discouraged by slips and omissions. Learn not to be so sensitive to failure that you just give up. Do not retreat from the podium in defeat. Do not give up so easily. Despite following all the useful tips given in this book, you may still forget an important point or make a blunder. Instead of admonishing yourself about it, put the matter behind you. Remind yourself that each presentation is a new opportunity to learn, a new possibility to reach out to listeners, a blank canvas on which you can draw whatever you want.

Remember that Churchill sat down in embarrassment after he tried giving a speech in the House of Commons from memory but forgot his lines. Remember that Churchill had a slight speech impediment, a lisp, which he overcame through sheer diligence and hard work. Remember that Churchill when he was a young army officer in India, at the age of twenty-three, wrote an article in 1897 called 'Scaffolding of Rhetoric', which remained unpublished because he could not find a publisher for it. Churchill overcame all these impediments to become one of the greatest speakers of the twentieth century.

## SHASHI THAROOR

At a debate on 28 May 2015 hosted by the Oxford Union, on the British colonization of India, Congress MP and writer Shashi Tharoor brilliantly argued that Britain owes reparations for its exploitation of the subcontinent. The motion for the debate was: 'This house believes Britain owes reparations to her former colonies' and Tharoor, along with other eminent speakers, spoke in favour of it. The video of the debate went viral on social media and within a week of the speech, it became Oxford Union's fifth most-watched YouTube video. It was Tharoor's 'rapier barbs' that got everyone's attention, such as the line, 'No wonder the sun never set on the British Empire, even God couldn't trust the English in the dark.'

Tharoor's speech is worthy of serious study by all students of public speaking, not only for its content but also for its eloquence, articulation, and rhetorical style—infused with passion, wit, humour—and for its use of analogies, quotations, and picture words.

## ALEXANDRIA OCASIO-CORTEZ

I end this chapter with a reference to a special public speech that should be a model for all students because it captures the essence of all that a good speech should be. This is a speech by a twenty-nine-year-old Hispanic American woman, a former bartender, who was elected to the United States Congress in 2019. Alexandria Ocasio-Cortez's address to the US House of Representatives on 23 July 2020 is a model of what a speech should be: eloquent, lucid, truthful, intelligent, moving, and persuasive.

Ocasio-Cortez's address is a masterpiece of plain, heartfelt speech that employs the tools of the orator, the rhetorician, and the preacher. What impressed me was her use of anaphora, repetition, rhythm, emphasis, cadence, and enunciation, and the seamless transition from idea to idea. In public speaking classes, students might like to study Ocasio-Cortez's speech, which has been widely tweeted and viewed on YouTube and other social media platforms.

## FINALLY

The art or skill of public speaking is not a gift from heaven, but rather an accomplishment achieved through hard work, countless drills, and hours and hours of practice. Next time you hear a brilliant speech, remember that the speaker in all probability has put in innumerable hours of relentless rehearsals. You, too, can achieve this level of competence, if not mastery, by adopting the suggestions and tips offered here. *Read this book and go for it!*

CHAPTER 64

# HOW TO CHAIR A SESSION

*The Chair can Set the Mood and Atmosphere of the Session*

## PERSONAL EXAMPLE

I have had the privilege of chairing many presentations, but my favourite remains the joint seminar in Chandigarh hosted by the Institute of Chartered Accountants of India and the Institute of Company Secretaries of India in 1995 (ICAI and ICSI, Chandigarh, 1995). The keynote speaker was S.K. Tuteja, former IAS officer with a fine service record with the Government of Punjab in various capacities. One of the panel speakers was Mohandas Pai, former CFO and board member of Infosys Limited.

Based on my experience, I recommend the following proven steps and procedures for successfully chairing a session.

## PRE-SESSION

Contact the speakers or panellists before the conference, introduce yourself, and ask them if they have any questions about their presentation. Ask them to give you a short biography, curriculum vitae, or résumé, so that you can introduce them properly at the event. Arrange to meet the speakers early at the conference and well before the session, so that you can both build a rapport with each other. Seek to establish empathy and harmony with them, and a friendly and comfortable bond.

## HOMEWORK

A certain amount of preparation is necessary both on the topic under discussion and on the background of the speakers. Do not expect to chair the session if you are clueless about the subject. Knowledge of the speakers' professional experience, credentials, and accomplishments is essential. This means not only getting their names right (including the correct pronunciation), but also knowing their designations and titles, their honorifics and awards, and their interests and passions.

## SESSION FORMAT

While the schedule, overall allocation of time, and the order of the speakers are given in the conference programme, it can be very helpful to spend some time preparing the format of the session. For example, try to think about a general introduction to the session and to all the speakers collectively, as well as specific introductions to each speaker, and decide whether questions will bc taken after each presentation, or at the end, after all the presentations have been completed.

## BE FIRM

Begin the session promptly and make sure that each speaker is given the same amount of time. No matter how awkward or difficult this may be, you must keep people to their allotted time. Cut off long-winded speakers politely but firmly. Do not let one speaker dominate and hog all the attention.

## INTRODUCING THE TOPIC

Take possession of your territory. Lean forward towards the audience and use the golden word 'you'. Make sure that in the initial phase, you make eye contact with the audience to get their attention and to introduce the topic under discussion. Do not assume that everyone is familiar with the topic. Keep your introductory remarks brief and to the point. Do not try to steal the thunder from the speakers.

Pep up your brief introduction with a suitable example, illustration, anecdote, story, or even a joke. You may also pick up something from recent newspaper headlines that is relevant to the topic under discussion. Be specific and concrete. Do not be abstract and vague. Avoid generalities and cliches. If you are visiting another city for chairing the session, it may be appropriate to make a few relevant remarks about the city to establish a rapport with the audience who are likely to be all local people.

## INTRODUCING THE SPEAKERS

Be brief, pertinent, accurate, and respectful in your introduction. Personalize the introduction to each speaker by giving specific details about them. If you know the speaker and have something complimentary or interesting to say about them, share it with the audience. Tell the audience something about the speaker's expertise, experience, accomplishments, and interests. This will help establish their credibility with the audience and make the session more enjoyable for both the audience and the speakers.

## COORDINATING THE DISCUSSION

After the presentations, announce that the floor is open for discussion and explain the structure and format of the Q&A session. It is necessary that you have total control over the procedure and discussion. It is also a good idea to request members of the audience asking questions to give their name and affiliation.

To set the ball rolling, you could ask the first question. If there are just a few questions from the audience, do not artificially extend the session in the hope of eliciting more questions. If there are too many questions, or if the questions are too difficult to understand or answer, or if the questions are too long and rambling, you may step in and remind the audience that specific issues can be discussed after the session, one-on-one with individual speakers. Sometimes questions from the audience can turn into meandering observations or mini presentations. It is your responsibility to keep this under control, and to interrupt the questioner if necessary.

## CLOSING THE SESSION

It is good practice for the session chair to sum up the proceedings after the last presentation rather than let the speakers and the audience discover that the session is over because the session chair has left the stage without saying anything. All you need to do is summarize the contents, or the main points or conclusions, of the session in a few sentences and offer a final thank you to all the speakers and to the audience for their participation.

## BEING ATTENTIVE

As the chair, listen attentively and make notes on relevant points that can be used to ask questions or to initiate a discussion later. Do not fidget or yawn. Do not slouch in your chair. In short, adopt proper body posture. Show your keen interest and involvement in the event by being attentive and alert.

## SMILE

Learn to smile and relax. A frown or scowl, or an otherwise unfriendly and aloof demeanour, will set the wrong tone. If you have forgotten how to smile, or the reason for it, please read the chapter 'Smile' in this book.

## HUMOUR

As the chair, use this opportunity to engage in some humour, wit, and repartee to elicit laughter, exclamations, and applause. Include some soft moments and light banter, which helps build a rapport with both the audience and the speakers. This serves as an ice-breaker and puts everyone at ease.

## BODY LANGUAGE

Convey through your body language that you mean to conduct the session in a manner that will add value to the discussion. Supplement your vocal message with smiles, eye contact, stance, choreography, hand gestures, and facial expressions.

## OVERALL

*The chair can set the mood and atmosphere of the session* by his attitude and behaviour: exude energy and authority, build audience awareness, establish eye contact, adopt a confident stance, and use humour. Do not let the mood be dry and humourless. Instead, build a relaxed and friendly atmosphere, marked by laughter and fun, bonhomie and warmth.

CHAPTER 65

# MAGIC LIST FOR EXCELLENCE IN PUBLIC SPEAKING

*Eight Important Techniques for Improving your Oratorical Skills*

## EIGHT IMPORTANT TECHNIQUES

The chapters in this book set out numerous methods for enhancing your public speaking skills and doing so with confidence, elan, and style. To deliver a brilliant speech, follow eight techniques, culled from this book, which play a key role in improving your oratorical skills. These are:

- Have a proper structure for your speech, with breaks, transitions, and recaps.
- Be specific and concrete, building your speech like a layer cake by incorporating examples, illustrations, and suitable stories.
- Adopt a balanced stance.
- Establish eye contact.
- Deliver what appears to be an extempore speech, but one that is based on extensive preparation, with or without prompt cards.
- Develop flexibility in your voice.
- Understand the importance of words and rhetorical devices.
- Practise, practise, practise.

The combination of these eight techniques will dramatically improve your ability to deliver an engaging and interesting speech, one that your audience will long remember. This then is my magic list for excellence in public speaking—proper structure, specifics, balanced stance, eye contact, extempore speech based on extensive preparation, flexibility in voice, words and rhetorical devices, and relentless practice.

## THREE FUNDAMENTAL PILLARS

Three out of these eight techniques will enable you to lay a solid foundation for successful speaking. These are my three fundamental pillars:

- *Be specific and concrete*, building your speech like a layer cake by incorporating suitable examples, apt illustrations, and pertinent stories. At times we tend to be more oriented towards facts and figures, numbers and data, but for me personally, stories, examples, and illustrations are essential for my style of speaking and I know that this is one of the major ways of really connecting with my audience. I am pleasantly surprised how some of my examples, illustrations, and stories are remembered even years after my speech.
- *Deliver what appears to be an extempore speech*, but one based on extensive preparation, with or without prompt cards. No matter how satisfactory your content may be, to read out the speech word by word from your notes is a deal breaker for me. Except for a few talks right at the beginning of my speaking career or eulogies delivered at memorials, I have hardly ever read out a speech. Think back to your favourite teacher at school or recall speakers at conferences who impressed you. This individual was probably someone who was enthusiastic, sincere, and

animated, someone who made a powerful vocal and visual impact. You will not be able to make a similar impression on your audience if you merely read your script.

Other than a few, all my speeches have been delivered extempore with notes, usually prompt cards. Over a period of time, I cut down the material jotted down on my prompt cards so that now they are just a few words for each thought. Lately, I have even stopped using prompt cards. I prepare the prompt cards, use them during my practice sessions and rehearsals, but do not carry them for the speech.

- *Practise, practise, practise* your speech so that it appears extempore. Insufficient practice, lack of rehearsal, or shoddy preparation are non-starters. I firmly believe that to be a powerful public speaker, you have to rehearse, rehearse, rehearse. The purpose of my rehearsals is not to memorize what I am going to say, but rather to become thoroughly familiar with the key points and the flow of ideas. I put in a lot of relentless practice. For me, a minimum of twelve training sessions from the time that my final prompt cards are ready is a prerequisite. For me, the magic number is generally twelve. The magic number for you may be four or twenty or anything in between. In any event, rehearse until the speech seems almost to come by itself, seemingly without too much effort or striving. When my audience analysis indicates too many unknowns, I increase the number of my drills. I only stop practising when I have reached a certain rhythm and fluency.

Lay a solid foundation for successful public speaking by mastering these three fundamental pillars. If you overload your speech with abstract concepts (instead of including specifics); if you read your speech out mechanically (instead of delivering what appears to be an extempore speech); and if you speak off the cuff, without sufficient rehearsal (instead of repeated practice), you will undercut your chances of success. Indeed, you will be guilty of self-sabotage. Including specifics, delivering what appears to be an extempore speech, and practising thoroughly are my three fundamental pillars for successful speechmaking, and the absence of any one of these will limit your chances of delivering a compelling and interesting speech.

## FINALLY

I end this chapter with an astute observation by Churchill from his unpublished article 'Scaffolding of Rhetoric', which he wrote in 1897 at the age of twenty-three while serving as an army officer in India: 'Of all the talents bestowed upon men, none is so precious as the gift of oratory. He who enjoys it wields a power more durable than that of a great king. He is an independent force in the world.'